encountering Christ

Stories of 12 Women
Who Walked and Talked
With Jesus

ANDREA ADAMS

FREILING
PUBLISHING

Published by Freiling Publishing,
a division of Freiling Agency, LLC.

70 Main Street, Suite 23-MEC
Warrenton, VA 20186

www.FreilingPublishing.com

Library of Congress Control Number: 2019911391

ISBN 9781950948109

Printed in the United States of America

This book is dedicated to my daughters Jess, Samantha and Valerie who survived the embarrassing moments I caused during their teen years to become the accomplished women they are today. I hope they are almost as proud of me as I am of them. A special thanks to Samantha without whose Facebook-ing, this dream of mine would never have become a reality.

TABLE OF CONTENTS

INTRODUCTION

This book is the culmination of twenty years of a Biblical storytelling ministry. It began when I took a class on church drama for my certification as a United Methodist Lay Speaker. One of the assignments was to portray a person from the Bible in a five-minute monologue. I chose Mary the Mother of Christ at the Cross. The class was moved to tears. After that, I began receiving requests to come and perform the story at many different churches. The ministry had begun. Many other women of the New Testament had stories which spoke to my heart, and so I added to the ministry. The hemorrhaging woman's courage and faith had always moved me, so she made an appearance not long after Mary. I had always thought Martha had received unfair criticism since she was giving to Jesus from her heart, just as her sister. I wanted her side of the story to be told. She is a fun one to do, and many women who hear her identify closely with her. And so, the ministry grew. It was a remarkable journey of which to be a part. I never advertised, don't have a website, and yet it has grown far beyond anything I ever imagined simply through word of mouth. Truly, it is blessed by God.

The twelve women whose stories are told here come from all walks of life, with all kinds of problems and all kinds of needs. Some already had deep faith, like Mary and Elizabeth. Their challenge was to live that faith in a society of doubters. Some had physical problems like the hemorrhaging woman and the hunched over woman. They found health and a new life. Others were outcasts such as the woman at the well and the Canaanite woman. They found acceptance and a future with hope. The sinful woman had given up on God, but He hadn't given up on her. Their one common factor was that they all searched for deeper meaning and someone to believe in. That someone was and is Jesus. He met them where they were but didn't leave them there. He offered hope, purpose and joy. He does the same with us today. Those who respond as these women did will find the same blessings. He is truly at the heart of this ministry.

I know God works through these stories. One incident stands out above all others for me. I was doing the woman at the well at an assisted living home. After I was finished, the activities coordinator told me this story: The woman in the front row was in their Alzheimer unit. Ever since she had been admitted, there was something bothering her, but she could never tell them what it was. She walked out of the service with tears of joy streaming down her face because she said, "Now I know I'm right with God."

I stood there in utter amazement. I silently thanked God for using me to touch her, and for letting me know He had used me. It was a moment for which I am eternally grateful. It is also the reason for this book. I didn't want these stories to die when I can no longer perform them.

The stories are easy to perform. All that is needed is a costume, except for Elizabeth who uses a party noise maker. I would suggest that you not just read them to an audience. It is much more fun to "become" the woman, interacting with the audience when possible. One other suggestion: always begin with prayer. I always take time to pace, shake and pray! It truly helps.

The most frequent compliment I get is, "I felt like I was with Jesus." What more can a woman ask than to be able to put someone in the presence of Christ. As you perform them, or just read them, I pray that your own encounter with Him will be life changing.

I want to thank my daughters who taught me about God as parent, their spouses, and especially my grandchildren who are a new generation of blessings. Thank you for all the times you lifted my spirit and for rejoicing with me as this book became a reality. I love you all.

Special thanks go out to my Thursday morning Bible study sisters who have been encouraging, supportive and powerful prayer warriors for me. I could ask for no better companions on this journey. You are all gifts from God.

Finally, the biggest thanks of all to our Lord Jesus. He gave me a vivid imagination, a talent for telling stories, a voice that can be heard and a way to use all these things for His glory. Praise be to God. He has truly blessed me abundantly.

ELIZABETH

Luke 1: 5-25

(*Elizabeth enters holding something behind her back.*)
I have something to show you. (*She takes out and
blows into a party noisemaker.*) Surprise! (*She blows
into it again.*) I just love these things. We didn't have
anything like this in my day and age. It doesn't look
like anything special, until someone fills it with breath.
(*She blows in it again.*) Then, it does surprising things.
I've known people like that. They don't look like
anything special, until God fills them with His breath,
(*blowing in it again*) and then they do surprising
things. (*Blows it again, and then puts the noisemaker
down.*)

But then, I have always believed we serve a God
of surprises. I myself was one of His surprises, and
not a very pleasant one according to my parents. They
seemed to take great delight in telling me just how
unwelcome I really was. Now I know that sounds
harsh, but in a way, it was good because it gave me
a special relationship with God. You see, I always
figured that if my own parents didn't want me in this
world, God must have a pretty good reason for having
created me. It just took me a long time to figure out

what that reason was. Also, it helped me see God in places other people didn't necessarily see Him. For instance, I love sunrises: the way the sky turns silver with little flashes of pink and yellow as the sun creeps up over the horizon. It is as if the whole day lies before you, a beautiful gift from God. A gift full of surprises: some pleasant and some not so pleasant. But even the not so pleasant ones can be made to work for good in the hands of God. Then there are the sunsets, with all the reds and oranges: it's like a warm blanket God wraps around you at the end of a busy day so you can rest safe and secure and awake renewed, ready for another gift full of surprises.

However, I learned early on not to share such musings with just anyone. People would look at me like I was some kind of a nut. I had one friend, though, Zechariah. He and I could talk about anything. Zech would sit and listen and think about it, (*in a deeper voice each time Zechariah speaks*) "Yes, Elizabeth, I see what you're saying. Very good."

Zech even went against the traditions of our society and taught me how to read and write. "Elizabeth," he said, "You have a good sharp mind, and God doesn't expect you to waste it. Come, I'll teach you to read."

I was thrilled. It opened up a whole new world for me!

When we reached the age to be married, we were delighted that our parents agreed we would make the perfect couple. And why not? I was from the priestly tribe of Aaron, and he was from the priestly tribe of Abijah, and you put two priestly tribes together, and it is the cause for great rejoicing. As a matter of fact, the entire village came out to rejoice with us. We became known as Zechariah and Elizabeth, the righteous!

Oh, boy, what a terrible thing to do to a young couple. You see, righteous people have so many expectations laid upon them. Righteous people never have any problems. They never fight with one another. Righteous people certainly never get angry with God. And they are always blessed by God.

Well, I'm here to tell you that righteous people do indeed have problems, and they fight with one another. It's just that they never let those problems, or those arguments get in the way of their love. Instead they work through them with conversation and compromise. And righteous people even get angry with God. But they know that that anger never affects their love for Him, nor more importantly, His love for them. And so, they work through it with conversation, but never compromise. After all, how do you compromise with God? He's always right. And righteous people are indeed blessed by God, just not always in the way society thinks they should be blessed.

Now, in my day, children were looked upon as blessings from God. The more God blessed you, the more children you had. So Zech and I looked forward to having a very large family. But it didn't happen. Every month we would pray about it, and we would get our hopes up, and every month those hopes would be dashed. As the months turned into years, my frustrations began grow. Each time I helped another mother birth a child, a mother already so worn down by too much responsibility that she wept at the thought of another mouth to feed, my heart would cry out, " Why her, Lord? Why didn't You give that baby to me? You know how much I want one."

But the still small voice would say, " Be patient, Elizabeth, the time is not right."

And in my day, an unwanted child, especially one born with a birth defect would be left out in the wilderness to die. When I would hear of one such child, my heart would cry out, "Why didn't you give that babe to me, Lord? Even that child I would have loved! "

But the still small voice said, " Trust Me, Elizabeth, I have something better in mind."

As the years turned to decades, the term "Zechariah and the Elizabeth, the righteous," took on far more of a tone of ridicule than respect, and the flame of hope of me ever being a mother burned down until it was nothing more than an ember. An ember by the name of Sarah, for Sarah, too, had been an old woman when granted her first-born son. But who am I compared to Sarah?

Zech, to his credit, never openly blamed me. Oh, he could have. He could have divorced me, for barrenness was grounds for divorce. But Zech loved me too much, and he trusted God too much. Still, there were times when I would catch him looking at me with a question in his eyes, "Is it she, Lord? Is there something wrong in her?"

However, Zech had his own flame of hope which took a long time to be realized. You see, because of the number of priestly tribes, each tribe could serve

in the Temple in Jerusalem for only two weeks out
of the year. Because of the number of priests in each
priestly tribe, the honor of serving as High Priest, of
being the one to go into the Holy of Holies to offer up
the prayers and incense on behalf of all of Israel, that
honor was chosen by lot. So, every year we would go
up to Jerusalem with our hopes high that this would
be the year Zech's lot would be drawn. And every year
we would come home disappointed. Then the question
in Zech's eyes would turn inward, "Is it I, Lord?
Is there something wrong in me?" As the decades
passed, Zech's flame of hope burned down until it was
nothing more than an ember: an ember by the name
of Abraham, for Abraham, too, had been an old man
when called upon to make a special sacrifice to God.

Then it happened.

We had gone to Jerusalem as usual. As we walked
to Temple that morning, the sunrise was even more
glorious than ever. The sky practically shimmered
in silver, the rays of the rising sun bouncing off the
Temple making it look like a living flame. It was so
beautiful; it took my breath away. I commented on it
to Zech.

"Yes, Elizabeth," he said, " I've been thinking the
same thing. Look how the Temple sparkles; a beautiful
gift from God. Perhaps today, Elizabeth, perhaps today
that gift will hold a pleasant surprise."

But the enthusiasm had gone out of his voice, and
I was afraid Zech's flame of hope was about to go out
completely, so my heart cried out, "Oh please, Lord,
please grant Your servant Zechariah this one reward.
You know how much he loves You. You know how

hard he tries to serve You. Please give him this one gift: let him serve as High Priest just once in his life."

The still small voice said, "Trust Me, Elizabeth." Then I thought I heard Him chuckle.

Zech went and joined the other priests. Low and behold, his lot was drawn! My heart rejoiced, "Oh, thank you, Lord. Thank you for giving Zech this gift."

But the still small voice said, "Oh, Elizabeth, you haven't seen anything yet." And I thought I heard Him chuckle again.

When they dressed Zech in the robes of the High Priest, he was so excited he looked like a little boy again. As they tied the rope around him, the rope that was used only in the case of dire emergency to pull the priest out so no one else would go in and desecrate the Holy of Holies, as they tied that rope around him, his eyes met mine and he gave me the old thumbs up. My thoughts went out to him, "Have a ball, Zech, and remember everything so you can tell me all about it." Then, with one deep breath, Zech stepped behind the curtain and into the Holy of Holies.

Over the years, I had come to know the prayers that Zech would be offering in there. Oh, he had never openly taught them to me, but he had practiced them so often that I was saying them right along with him. But the time passed when he should have been finished, but he didn't come out. The "what-if vultures" began circling. What if something happened to him in there? What if this was all too much for him? But I quickly shooed them away thinking, "No, he's just taking his time, enjoying the moment, for he'll never have another one like it."

However the time for that to be a valid excused passed also and the "what-if vultures" came back in force when I saw the priests talking among themselves, "Do you think we ought to pull on the rope? Zech was an old man, you know."

Just as they got rope taught, Zech stepped out from behind the curtain, out of the Holy of Holies, but he didn't say the words all of Israel was waiting to hear. He didn't say anything at all. He just pushed past the priests and signaled for me to join him. As I ran up, I said, "Zech, what's wrong? What happened in there?"

He started going like this. (*Flapping arms*)

"A bird, Zech? You saw a bird in there?"

(*Shake your head. Point to the sky, circle your head, flap arms.*) "An angel. You saw an angel in there. (*Nod head*) Well, what did the angel say?"

(*Rock arms like holding a baby.*) "A baby. The angel told you somebody's going to have a baby?"

(*Nodding your head.*) "Well, who's going have a baby, Zech?" And he pointed at me.

"Oh, no, Zech! You know that's not possible. (*Stomping feet and pointing to sky.*) Yes, Zech, I know with God all things are possible, but a baby? Me?!"

And the still small voice said, "Surprise!" and started to laugh.

I said, "Zech, let's go home. You can calm down and tell me all about it."

Well, we went home, and I was very glad Zech had taught me how to read because it was the only way he could communicate with me. He got a big slate and some charcoal and started writing down everything he had seen in there. My Zech had indeed seen an angel. Not just any angel, mind you, but Gabriel. Gabriel! One of the archangels who dwell in the very throne room of heaven waiting to fly with wings of an eagle to earth with messages for poor mortals from the Lord God Almighty Himself. That Gabriel appeared to my Zech. He told Zech that we were indeed to have a child. A son. And we were to name him John.

Oh great, I've waited all these years to have a baby and now I don't even get to name him. But that's all right. John's a perfectly nice name. There are no Johns in the family. People are going to think it's a little weird, but I can deal with that.

Well, our John is to be a prophet.

(*Sarcastically*) Wonderful! I know Israel's history with her prophets, and it is not a pretty sight. But if that's what God wants, then that's what God gets.

John is to be a prophet and he is to call the people of God to a new repentance. In addition, he is to baptize them in water.

Better and better! My son John, the prophet and the baptizer. But he is to baptize the people of God in order to prepare their hearts and minds for the coming of the, (*as an aside*) are you ready for this? The Messiah. The Messiah! The promised one of God! The Messiah who will bring down the powers that lord it over us and lift His people up into a new kingdom. And my son John is to be the herald for that new kingdom. Because Zech did not believe what Gabriel had told him, he had been struck mute and would remain that way until John was born and circumcised and consecrated.

And ladies, I must be perfectly honest with you, my first thought was, " Nine months of peace and quiet, oh thank you, Lord!" But I quickly repented of that, "I'm sorry, Lord, I really didn't mean it quite like that."

The still small voice just chuckled, "It's all right, Elizabeth. I understand. Consider this My gift to you and use it wisely."

Well, my body did indeed begin to show signs of a pregnancy, but I had known other women who had so desperately wanted a child that their bodies showed all the signs without there actually being a baby there. Is that what was happening to me? Or worse, was this a tumor growing within me that would eventually take my life? Oh, there were little flutterings down there, but they could easily be dismissed as gas. Is this really a baby?

And if it is, will my son ever get to meet this Messiah whose coming he is to foretell, or is He still generations and generations away?

And if he would get to meet this Messiah, does that mean that right now there is another woman receiving a similar message of a promise growing within her: A promise so powerful that this world will never be the same again?

And if there is such a woman, then what must she be like?

Let me see, what do the prophets say? A virgin shall give birth to a son. All right, a virgin: young, unmarri...(*stop with a shocked and worried look*)

Oh, my dear Lord, a young unmarried girl giving birth in my day and age?! Why, she could be stoned to death! Oh, how frightened she must be. How alone she must feel. Oh, Lord, if only I knew who she was, I could help her. I could mentor her. At the very least Zech and I could protect her. Oh, if only I knew.

That day dawned gray and rainy. The aches and pains of getting out of bed were even more pronounced than usual. I remember thinking, "Not a day for pleasant surprises."

As I worked, I heard a small noise behind me. I turned and there stood my young cousin Mary, drenched to the bones. Her hair and her gown were dripping wet. She was shivering, but I'm not sure if it was from cold or fear, for she looked for all the world like a poor little frightened, half-drowned kitten.

Yet, in her eyes there was a gleam, a sparkle of a secret well hid. A secret so awesome she was afraid to let it out for fear of the consequences. In an instant, I knew she was the one. I threw my arms open to her and she came running towards me releasing a torrent of tears of relief. As she came, I felt within me a kick, so pronounced, there was no longer any question. This was not my imagination, this was not a tumor, this was not gas. This was a baby.

As I wrapped my arms around her, I felt the power of the Holy Spirit around us and within us, for when our tummies touched our sons moved towards one another, mine dropping as if to his knees. Somehow, I knew it would always be this way: my son the lesser to hers, me the lesser to Mary.

I pulled back and looked at her, "Oh Mary, Mary, who am I that I should be visited by the mother of our Lord?"

"You know, Elizabeth!" she cried. "Oh, Elizabeth, isn't it wonderful what God is doing?

"He has heard the cries of His people Israel. He has remembered the covenant He made with our ancestors, with Abraham, Isaac, and Jacob, and He is sending us His Messiah.

"His Messiah, who will open the eyes of all those who have been blind to God that all may see Him in His glory.

"His Messiah, who will lift the burdens of those so weighted down by the cares and concerns of this world that they merely limp through life and cause them to dance.

"He will feed us on manna from heaven and let those satisfied with the riches of earth go hungry.

"He will break the chains of sin which enslave us and set us free to rejoice in His service.

"He will bring down the high and mighty who lord it over us and lift His people up into a new kingdom; a kingdom over which He Himself will reign graciously and eternally.

"And look who He has chosen to accomplish this magnificent feat. Me, Elizabeth, He has chosen me, the lowliest of the lows. He has chosen me to prove that God can take the least and do the most with it. And from now all generations will call me blessed because I have been chosen to serve the Lord."

Now, Zech was over in a corner taking all of this in, and for the next several weeks he worked feverously on something, but he would never show us what he was working on. Finally, he came and presented Mary with a small scroll. She couldn't read, so she gave me the honor of reading it to her. Here, Zech had taken her simple words of praise and crafted them into a beautiful psalm. A psalm that as I read it brought tears to my eyes. A psalm that I knew would be handed down from generation to generation. A psalm which you can read in your scriptures to this day. Yet, with as beautiful as that psalm is, I have always thought that God was even more pleased with the simple words of praise which flowed forth from Mary's lips unscripted and unrehearsed. You see, I have always believed that we serve a God who hears, not so much with His ears, but rather with His heart. How else could He maneuver His ways through our tangled web of wants and get to the heart of our needs? How else could He discern between words of duty and those of love?

Well, Mary stayed with us and we did indeed form a bond; a bond that neither the difference in our ages nor time nor distance would ever be able to break. After all, we were two women unique in the annals of history: mother of a prophet and mother of the Messiah. As I watched Mary, for the first time in my life I was very grateful for my age because I knew I would never live to see what society does to my son. But Mary? Oh, my dear Lord, Mary is so young she will see it all. She will hear every word He preaches; see every miracle He performs. She will know the adoration of the crowd and watch as those cheers turn to jeers. She will see Him betrayed, arrested, beaten, convicted on false charges and then stand by helplessly watching Him die the death of a criminal, slowly and painfully on the cross.

Oh, my dear Lord, please grant this gentle soul the strength she will need to bear such a sword. Grant her too, Lord, the joy of being there that morning when You break now and forever the gates of hell. Let her witness that stone being rolled away. Let her see her Son walk out of that tomb resurrected and glorified to take His place on the throne next to you. Grant her that moment of joy also.

And the still small voice said, " Trust Me, Elizabeth, I shall do all you ask for Mary."

Mary, fortunately, was too young to see that far into the future. Besides, she had more pressing concerns on her mind, the foremost of which was Joseph. "He doesn't believe me, Elizabeth," she cried.

I said, "Well, Mary, you have to admit it is a rather unbelievable story. I mean, conceived by the Holy Spirit? Come on, give the guy a break."

"Oh, but he should know I'd never lie to him. How am I ever going to convince him I'm telling the truth?"

"You're not going to, dear. You're going to leave it to God. I don't know how He'll do it, but He'll do it. Or maybe God doesn't expect you to be married. Maybe He expects you to raise His Son on your own. If He does, He will give you the strength and the means with which to do it, because what God expects us to do, He will enable us to do. Still, I think that God knows the importance of a father in a boy's life; someone to teach him and to show him what it means to be a man. But maybe it's not Joseph."

We began to study the scriptures and we found that the Messiah is to be born in Bethlehem.

"Bethlehem!" cried Mary, " Oh but Elizabeth, we live in Nazareth. Even if I can convince Joseph to marry me, how am I ever going to talk him into moving to Bethlehem?"

I said, "You're not going to, dear, you're going to leave it to God. I don't know how He'll do it, but He'll do it. Maybe that's your answer. Maybe Joseph isn't the man God has chosen for you. Maybe there is some man in Bethlehem He's chosen, and He will bring the two of you together and you will love him tremendously."

"Oh no," she said, "I could never love anyone but Joseph."

"Mary," I said, "what God expects us to do, He will enable us to do."

"Oh, but I want Joseph!"

"I know you do dear, but our wants and God's don't always go hand in hand. Look at me, I always wanted a baby, but never in my wildest dreams did I expect to be having one at my age. I don't know if I can handle this physically or emotionally. You've heard the way they talk about me out there. But I know that this child is perfect in the plans of God and I trust that what He expects me to do, He will enable me to do. You must learn to trust Him like that also."

We studied a little further and learned that the Messiah is to come out of Egypt.

"Egypt!" cried Mary, "Oh, Elizabeth, I don't want to go to Egypt! Egypt is too big. It's too pagan! I'm scared of Egypt!"

I said, "Mary dear, calm down. You know you're not going to be going there alone. God will be with you. He's not going to let anything happen to His Son or to you. Trust Him. What God expects us to do, He will enable us to do."

One day as we were working Zech came in with a very enigmatic smile on his face. I said, "What's up, Zech?"

He pointed outside. "We have a visitor?"

(*Nod head.*)

"Well, show him in."

Zech stepped to the side and in walked Joseph. As his eyes locked on Mary, he uttered the three most beautiful words I have ever heard, "I believe you."

Mary went rushing into his arms and they kissed so tenderly. Zech came over and put his arms around me and kissed me tenderly. It may be blasphemy, but I don't think the presence of the Holy Spirit could be felt any more powerfully in the Holy of Holies than it was in my kitchen at that moment.

Joseph explained what had happened. "Mary," he said, "I love you, but I have to admit I didn't believe you. I mean, conceived by the Holy Spirit? I was making plans to put you away. Oh, I never would have let them stone you, and I would have provided for you, but not as my wife. Then one night Gabriel came to me. Gabriel, Mary! He told me that you would never lie to me. He told me I could believe everything you said. He said the Baby is that of the Holy Spirit and he said I should marry you and raise the Child as my own. Now, Mary, I love you almost as much as I love

God, and I will do as He says. But I have to tell you both, I am scared out of my wits! I mean, how am I supposed to be father to the Father?"

She took his hands in hers and said, "It's all right, Joseph. I understand. I'm scared too. I mean, mother of the Messiah! But I know that what God expects us to do, He will enable us to do, and I think you will make a wonderful father." Then she looked at me and gave me a little wink.

Mary and Joseph stayed with us until John was born. Mary even helped with the delivery. John came into this world kicking and screaming. I remember looking up at Mary and saying, "Well, he certainly has the voice for crying in the wilderness. "And ladies, I have to tell you, there were times in the weeks that followed I really wished he were crying in the wilderness instead of in my bed. But each time I would think such a thing, I would quickly repent, "I'm sorry, Lord, I really didn't mean that."

And the still small voice would say, "It's all right, Elizabeth. I know how difficult this is for you, but I am here, and I will provide for all your needs."

And He did.

On the eighth day we took John to be circumcised and consecrated. When the time came for the all-important question to be asked, the priests looked to me because Zech still couldn't speak. "What is the name of this child?"

I very proudly responded, "His name is John."

"John? Zechariah, there are no John's in your family. Don't you want the baby named after you?"

Well, Zech got his big slate and wrote in very large letters, (*writing on an invisible slate*) "His name is John." Underlined, (*making a swishing noise and underlining on the invisible slate*) Exclamation point! (*writing 3 exclamation points with swishing sounds*)

And so, the baby was named John. As soon as he was, Zech got his voice back and broke into a psalm he had written for himself; a psalm you can also read in your scriptures to this day. Now, I don't remember everything Zech said, because I was a bit preoccupied at the moment, but I do remember him saying that our son is not the true light of God, but merely a reflection of that light; someone to point the way to the true light of God. Isn't that what should truly be said of all of us?

Mary and Joseph left shortly thereafter to return to Nazareth. Yes, Nazareth. Mary's last words to me were, "I can't get him to move to Bethlehem. How am I ever going to get him to go to Bethlehem?"

I said, "You're not going to, dear. You're going to leave it to God. I don't know how He'll do it, but He'll do it. What God expects us to do, He enables us to do."

Sure enough, a little while later, I figured Mary had to have been in her eighth or ninth month, a decree went out from Caesar Augustus that all of the world should be taxed. Each man according to his heritage should return to the place of his ancestors to be registered and to pay that tax. Joseph, I knew, as was Mary, was from the house of David and that meant Bethlehem.

My thoughts went out that invisible bond and crashed into hers coming back at me," Ah, that's how He's going to do it."

A few weeks later, I had just gotten John in bed asleep and I went out to look at the night sky. You see, in addition to sunrises and sunsets I have also always loved the night sky. In my day it was believed the stars were actually angels who spent the night singing the praises of God.

That night the stars seemed especially vivid and sparkling. I remember looking up and thinking, "Wow, the angels are really singing God's praises tonight."

Then, all of sudden the biggest, brightest and most beautiful star I have ever seen burst into view. I thought, "Wow, that angel is really proud; almost like a father at the birth of his first born so... Oh, my dear Lord, Mary's delivered. Jesus is born. Immanuel, God is with us. Oh, thank You Lord, and please take care of them. All three of them."

And the still small voice said, "I shall, Elizabeth, I shall!" and started to laugh.

Well, with great joy often comes great sorrow, and so it was with the birth of Jesus. Somehow, Herod found out about the young king and in his fear and jealousy decided to kill the boy before He could ever threaten his throne. He sent out his troops with orders to kill every child under the age of two.

I panicked. "Lord," I said, " Mary and Joseph are young enough to get Your Son to safety, but Zech and I are too old to run with John. You're going to have to protect him." So, I hid him, and I begged him to keep that strong voice of his quiet and I went out to stand guard with Zech.

Zech tried to reason with the soldiers not to carry out this odious order while I tried to comfort grieving mothers holding dead children in their arms, all the while praying for the safety of my own.

At one point a young soldier came up and started to push us aside. My heart cried out, " Oh, God, do something! "

At that very moment the man's commanding officer came by, " Boy, what is the matter with you? Can't you see these two are too old to have a child that age? Don't even bother with them. Come on. Let's just finish this abominable business and get out of here."

For the last time in my life I was very grateful for my age because I knew it had been that which had saved my son's life.

In the weeks that followed, I often wondered how Mary and Joseph had managed. Even the answer to that unspoken prayer came in a most surprising way: in the form of a young shepherd boy by the name of Hezekiah.

Hezzie came looking for us one day. As we fed him, because the poor child looked about half starved, he told us what had happened. "Yeah," he said, "We had been up there on the mountains watching our sheep when all of a sudden these angels appeared to us. They told us the Son of God had been born down there in Bethlehem and we should go and see Him. Well, we went down and, sure enough, there they were: Mary and Joseph and the Babe lying in a manger just like the angels said they'd be."

I said, "Wait a minute, Hezekiah, are you telling me the Son of God was born in a stable?"

The still small voice said, "Surprised, Elizabeth? Even nature needs a Redeemer."

Hezzie went on, "I was so impressed with this young family that I stayed on after the others had left so I could help out all I could. Joseph, he was teaching me carpentry so I could better myself. Then one day these really rich men came in. They were something. Their robes were fancier than Herod's himself. Well, they came in and they bowed down and they worshipped this Child. I thought, 'Huh, there we were the lowest of the low and here they are the highest of the high and we're all worshipping this same Baby.'"

"But then they told us that Herod was going to try and kill the boy so we had to get Him to safety. That's when Joseph remembered he has relatives in Egypt, so they gave them a whole bunch of gold and fancy incense and stuff they can sell later on, and they're off to Egypt. But Mary sent me to you, Elizabeth with this message. She told me to tell you, 'Ah, that's how He's going to do it.' She said you'd understand."

I said, "Yes, Hezekiah, I understand. Thank you."

Well, Hezzie stayed with us, and he became a big brother to John. Believe you me, with parents the ages of Zech and I John needed a big brother; someone to teach him the joys of being a little boy and how to survive in the wilderness. It all worked out very well. John got a big brother, Zech and I got the help we needed, and Hezzie got a family and a better life. So, even those unknown prayers were answered in a most surprising way.

But then, as I said, I believe we serve a most surprising God. That is my prayer for you this day; that you, too, come to know the God of all surprises. May you see Him in sunrises and sunsets. May you greet each day as a special gift. Accept the pleasant surprises with joy and thanksgiving, and wait on the not so pleasant ones, trusting that a God powerful enough to use even the hatred of Herod to accomplish His purposes can surely take the blackest of threads and weave them into the beautiful tapestry He has planned for your life. May you serve Him boldly, knowing that whatever He expects you to do, He will indeed enable you to do. And may you always have the peace, the joy, and the blessings that come with that knowledge.

Amen.

POINTS TO PONDER FOR ELIZABETH

Read Luke 1

1. How have you witnessed the God of surprises in your own life?

2. In what ways do you see Him in places others don't necessarily see Him?

3. What kind of a marriage did Zechariah and Elizabeth have?

4. How did not having a child for so long help or hurt their love? Their faith?

5. Zechariah becomes mute because of his lack of faith. How did that help convince Elizabeth that their child was a special child of God?

6. Have you ever felt ostracized because of some situation in your life?

7. How did God help you through that time?

8. Why did Mary go to see Elizabeth?

9. How does Elizabeth's faith help Mary's?

10. Think of a spiritual mentor you have had. How did that person help you grow your faith?

11. How have you been a mentor for someone else?

12. Read Luke 1: 46-55. What does this song of praise teach us about God and His relationship with His people?

13. Read Luke 1: 67-79. What does this tell us about John's role in salvation?

14. Do you agree with Elizabeth when she says we should all be a reflection of the true light, pointing the way to the true light?

15. How does your life reflect that belief?

16. In this story, Elizabeth tells us there were two times in her life that she was grateful for her age. When were they?

17. Why was she grateful at those times?

18. Matthew 2 tells us of Herod's plot to destroy the young King by killing all the babies. How did God use this hatred of Herod to accomplish His purposes?

19. Has there ever been a time in your life when something bad has helped God's purpose for you?

20. Elizabeth repeatedly says that what God expects us to do, He will enable us to do. Has there been a time in your life when you have done something only because God has helped you do it?

21. What were the results?

22. Read Elizabeth's benediction. How could following her advice improve your relationship with God?

23. How could it improve your outlook on life?

THE INNKEEPER'S WIFE

Luke 2: 1-7

(Enter from off-stage and call back to unseen boy)
Jethro! Jethro, boy! You go get those goats milked and
mind you don't wake Miss Mary or the Baby!

Oh my, such excitement at my place last night.
My name is Esther. My husband Simon and I run the
finest inn in all of Bethlehem. Now mind you, it is
not the biggest inn in all of Bethlehem. Nor it is the
fanciest inn in all of Bethlehem. But it is the finest inn
in all of Bethlehem. How do we know it's the finest
inn? Well, our customers tell us that. "Simon," they
say, "you run the finest inn in all of Bethlehem."

Now the reason our inn is considered so fine is
that when you stay with us, you're treated like family.
That means you get good food and plenty of it. You
get clean linens, which is not necessarily true of other
inns of my day. And you are guaranteed your safety,
which is also not necessarily true of other inns of my
day. The reason you can be assured of your safety is
because of my husband Simon. Simon the lion he's

known as. Partly because he has this head full of curly red hair and this nice full soft curly red beard that all in all gives the appearance of a lion's main, and partly because he is big and burly. If anyone dares to step out of line, well, my Simon is right there to make sure he is back in line immediately. And if perchance Simon isn't around, and a customer puts one finger wrong near one my children? (*Swinging an invisible broom*) Well, he's going to get the business end of my broom right up his a... anyway.

Our inn has been filled for weeks. Now the reason for this great upturn in business is that the Roman government in their infinite wisdom has decided to tax people just for being people. Can you imagine that, taxing a person just for being a person? Honestly, I think they would tax the very air we breathe if they could figure out how to do it. You probably don't have that problem with your government in this day and age but... (*reacting to the response from the audience*) Oh, maybe you do have that problem with your government in this day and age.

Huh, I guess that just goes to prove that the more things change, the more things stay the same. Well, be that as it may, somebody somewhere, had to have been a man, decided that the easiest way of doing this was for each man according to his heritage to return to the place of his ancestors to be registered and to pay this tax. None of us have been able to figure out for whom this is supposed to be easier. It certainly isn't easier for the people who have to travel.

It isn't easier for the tax collectors who have to keep track of all the comings and goings. It isn't even easier for those of us who run inns. Very profitable, yes, but easier, no. However, that is the reason we have been filled to overflowing for weeks.

Yesterday, I had just finished serving lunch and was sweeping out the inn thinking about what I was going to prepare for supper when I saw Simon talking to this lovely young couple and I'll tell you, my heart went out to that poor girl. There she was, riding on the back of that donkey, looking like she was about ready to deliver any minute now, and I thought some not very nice thoughts about the Roman government, because I didn't think anyone had the right to expect a child in her condition to travel anywhere, even if was just from two streets over. And I knew what Simon was telling them. He was telling them that we don't have any room for them. And he's right, we don't! I mean, we have people staying in parts of our inn now I didn't even know we had. But I just had the feeling we had to do something for this young couple.

Well, Simon comes back up to inn and he's shaking his head and muttering, (*in a deeper voice for Simon*) "Nazareth."

I said, "What?"

He said, " Nazareth. Those young people have come all the way from Nazareth, and I have to turn them away."

I said, "Nazareth? But, Simon, Nazareth is 80 miles from here. We can't just turn them away."

"Well, what am I supposed to do, Esther? I can't just throw out paying customers because you feel sorry for them."

I thought about for a moment and said, "Well, why don't we offer to let them stay in our stables?"

"Oh, Esther," he says, "I can't ask them to stay in our stables!"

"Well, why not, I'd like to know? Our stables are warm and dry and at least they'll have some privacy. And our stables are a darn sight cleaner than any inn their going to find in Bethlehem now, even if they could find one. Now you go back and ask them if they want to stay in our stables. If they say no that's their business. We'll at least know we've done all we could."

"But, Esther," he starts.

"Simon, what if that were our Hannah and her Benjamin? Wouldn't you want somebody to do something?"

Well, that got him. "All right, all right, I'll ask. Young sir, young sir."

I saw him talking to the young man. He looked at his wife and she nodded. Honestly, I think that poor little thing would have been willing to sleep on a bed of nails in the middle of the marketplace just to get off that donkey! Well, Simon got all excited. He grabbed the donkey's reigns, nearly knocking the poor girl off and starts up towards the stables. As they're passing the door of the inn, I hear him telling them, "Yeah, it's like I told the wife, our stables are warm and dry and at least you'll have some privacy."

Like I told the wife?! Oh, Lord love him, somebody has to! But I really didn't mind, because at least now I knew they would be safe and I was going to make darn sure they got some good food in them that night, even if I had to skimp on somebody else's.

So, I go into the kitchen and I start preparing dinner. The next thing I know Simon comes in and he's shaking his head again. "What's the matter now?"

"They wanted to pay me."

"Simon," I said, "You didn't take any money from those young people, did you?"

"Esther," he said, "I can't accept money for them staying in our stables. Besides, I don't think they have 2 coins to rub together." Joseph," (*in a normal voice as an aside*) that was the young man's name, his wife's name was Mary, "Joseph is a carpenter, so I told him we have some things around here that need fixing and he can do that in payment for staying in our stables. Jethro! Jethro, boy, go break something young Joseph can fix!"

Go break something? Well, that's my Simon. He may look like a lion, and he may roar like a lion, but deep inside he has the heart of a pussycat.

Well, I was more determined than ever to do all I could for this young couple. Now, my Hannah and her Benjamin have been married for pert nigh 2 years and there is not one sign of a grandchild on the way. I don't mean to tell the good Lord His business, but I see no reason why a healthy, loving, God-fearing couple like my Hannah and her Benjamin have not yet made me a grandma. I'm ready. They're ready. It seems the only one not ready is the Lord, and you can't very well argue with Him, can you? But whatever the reason, I have all these baby things just waiting for a grandchild that isn't coming, and so I decided I would give them to Mary. I made up a basket of food and a basket of baby things, and I was just getting ready to go up to stables when I remembered this gown that was just perfect for nursing, so I went to get it. When I got back, there was Simon standing next to the table looking at my two baskets, laughing at me.

"I thought one of the selling points was that they would have some privacy."

"Now, Simon," I said, "Nobody staying under our roof has ever gone hungry, and I don't intend to start now, even if that roof is just the roof or our stable. As for the baby things, well, you said you don't think they have much, and I'll have plenty of time to make more for Hannah, so I see no reason why I shouldn't give... "

He just held up his hands, "It's all right, Esther, it's all right. Just give the children my best."

Well, it wasn't until later that I found out exactly what he meant by that, but at the moment I didn't care. I just grabbed my 2 baskets and started up the hill towards the stables.

Now, I'm about half-way up when suddenly, the stable doors fly open, and out runs Joseph, his arms flailing, (*in a deeper voice for Joseph*)"Oh Mrs., Mrs., you've got to help! My wife's having a baby!"

"All right, dear, all right, calm down! I know your wife is having a baby. It's perfectly obvious your wife is having a baby."

(*In the deeper voice*)"No, you don't understand. She's having it right now!"

"All right, dear, all right, relax. Women have been having babies for centur...

"Oh, not like this one."

Now, isn't that just like youth? Doesn't matter how many generations have gone before them, no one has done it quite like they have. But, you know, that's good. I mean, as we get older, we tend to lose sight of all the miracles God performs in our lives each and every day. Take babies for instance. That first child is always greeted with such joy and wonder. "Oh, look at the baby. Look what God has done. What a miracle this is. Look, he has little fingernails and little toenails and everything. Oh, God is so good. Love is so grand. Oh, look, he just spit up! Isn't that cute?"

The second baby is pretty much the same way. "Oh, look, another baby. Isn't it wonderful what God has done? Look at all that dark curly hair he has. God is so good."

By the third and fourth baby it becomes more like, "Oh, we're having another baby. Isn't that (*pause and with a questioning voice*) nice?"

By the seventh and eighth, it becomes, "Oh Lord, here we go again." When in fact, that eighth baby is no less a miracle than that first baby was. And that eighth baby is no less a part of God's plan than that first baby was. It's just that we lost sight of that in the humdrum problems of day to day living, so we need that excitement and wonder of youth to open our eyes once more to all the blessings God continues to shower on us each and every day.

Oh, I'm sorry. I tend to get off on these tangents. Simon laughs at me, "Esther," he says, "You should have been a rabbi." Right! Like they are ever going let a woman be a rabbi!

Anyway, I got Joseph all calmed down. "Joseph, dear," I said, "I will go take care of Mary. I have had eight babies of my own, and I have helped birth dozens and dozens of others. You go find Simon. You tell him what's happening, and he will tell you exactly what you have to do."

He was off and running. I knew he was good hands. If there is one thing that husband of mine can do, it's talk. I'll tell you, he can talk about anything, anywhere, anytime, with anyone and I knew he would keep Joseph well occupied while Mary and I tended to the important task of bringing that child into this world.

When I got to the stable, I walked in and there stood Mary. The first words out of her mouth were, "Where's Joseph? Is he all right?"

"Yes, dear, Joseph is fine. I sent him to Simon. Simon will take good care of him while you and I tend to the important business of making sure his child is born safely."

"Oh, it's not Joseph's child."

"Dear, dear, that is none of my business! That is strictly between you and Joseph and God."

"Well, that certainly is true. After all, this is God's baby."

I just looked at her. "All babies are God's babies."

I gave her a little exam and I realized we had some time before things got really interesting, so I showed her the things I had brought. Oh, she got all excited over the baby things. I told her all about Hannah and Benjamin.

"Well," she said, "God must have a reason for not sending them a child."

"Oh, I'm sure He does. I just wish He'd let me in on it. I think life would be so much simpler if God would just tell us exactly what He expects of us."

She laughed a little. "I used to think that, too, but you know, Esther, when God does tell you exactly what He expects of you, it can be an awful responsibility."

I thought about it, and, you know, she's right. I mean, if I had known how long Simon's mother was going to be living with us, (*pausing and shaking head*) I might never have married him.

Then think of all the fun I would be missing out on. Don't get me wrong. It's not that I don't love the old woman. I just don't like her very much. She is so opinionated: thinks everything should be done her way and it's my house, for crying out loud!

Well, anyway, we started walking, and Mary started asking me some of the strangest questions. "Esther," she said, "Do you believe that God keeps His promises?"

I thought about it, and He's always taken care of me and mine, so I said, "Yes, Mary, I believe that God keeps His promises."

Then she said, "Well, do you believe He will keep the promises He made through the prophets? You know, about sending a Messiah?"

Well, between you and me and the gatepost, I have been so busy raising those eight little promises God's given me that I haven't had a whole lot of time to think about what He may or may not have promised through the prophets, but I wasn't about to tell her that. So, I said, "Yes, Mary, I believe that God will keep the promises He made through the prophets about sending a Messiah someday." Marvelous word "someday. "It's not really yes and it's not really a no, it's kind of non-committal. (*Speaking to invisible children*) "Yes, dear, we'll talk about getting another dog someday. Of course, darling, we see about buying a horse someday. Yes, my precious, we'll discuss you having your own room someday." Marvelous word "someday."

"Yes, Mary, I believe that God will keep the promises He made through the prophets about sending a Messiah someday."

Then she said, "What would you say if I were to tell you that this baby is the promised Messiah?"

Well, I fought back the urge to go running from stable screaming, "Simon, we've got a lunatic staying with us!" because she seemed like such a sweet sincere little thing. So, I swallowed hard and said, "To tell you the truth, Mary, I'd have a bit of problem with that. I mean, don't you think that if God were to send His Messiah, He would send Him to a rich and powerful family?"

She said, "Well, I've though a lot about that. You know, Esther, the Messiah isn't coming to establish a political kingdom. Rather, the Messiah is coming to draw all people to God. Now, it is much easier for a rich man to approach a poor man, than for a poor man to approach a rich man, so wouldn't it make more sense for the Messiah to be a poor man so more people would feel comfortable coming to Him?"

I thought about it, and, you know, she had a point in a weird sort of way. So, I said, "All right, Mary, I will accept the fact that God would send His Messiah to a poor family instead of a rich one so more people would feel comfortable coming to Him. But, Mary, don't you think God would have least provided a room for His Son to be born in?"

She said, "To tell you the truth, Esther, I am far more comfortable out here in this stable, with just you and these animals than I would be in any hot overcrowded inn with everybody gawking at me."

I had to admit she was right. It was pleasant in that stable last night. The moon was shining brightly. The temperature was just about perfect. And the animals seem to sense something important was happening. If I were a fanciful woman, I would swear they were talking to one another. The cows were gently mooing; the goats were quietly bleating; the doves up in the rafters were sweetly cooing; and that donkey? That donkey sounded like he was bragging about what he had done. But then, I am not a fanciful woman.

So I said, "All right, Mary, I will accept the fact that God would send His Messiah to a poor family instead of a rich one, and I will accept the fact that you are more comfortable out here than you would be in some hot overcrowded inn. But Mary, why on earth would God ever allow Simon and me to be part of such a wondrous event?"

She stopped dead in her tracks, and she looked at me and said, "Oh, Esther, how can you even ask such a question? Look at yourselves. Your inn was overcrowded, yet you found room for us. Your lives are overly busy, but you've taken time out to care for me and the Baby, and you've given me all these wonderful baby things for Him. And when I told you the Baby wasn't Joseph's you never even missed a beat. It didn't matter to you. I wish the people of Nazareth had been so understanding. Even my own parents look at me like I'm the world's greatest sinner and Joseph was a fool for having married me. But not you, it didn't matter to you. All that matters to you is me and the Baby. Now what more could God ask for His Son than to be welcomed into this world by such kind, generous, loving, non-judgmental arms?"

I was a little embarrassed. I was just doing what comes naturally. I've seen girls in that situation before, and usually it isn't their fault, and you certainly can't blame the baby. I really didn't know what to say, which is unusual for me. But as it turned out, I didn't need to say anything, because about that time, Mary went, "Whoa!" The water broke and we were into some serious labor.

Now, labor is a very good word for it because there is nothing more difficult than bringing a child into this world, and Messiah or no Messiah, Mary was no different than the rest of us. That poor little thing huffed and she puffed and she grunted and she groaned, and she pushed and she panted and she panted and she pushed until finally, out came the messiest, the wrinkliest, the ugliest most beautiful baby I have ever seen in all my born days. I held Him up, and I swatted His little bottom, and He let out such a cry, and everything stopped. The cows stopped mooing, the goats stopped bleating, the doves up the rafters stopped cooing, even the crickets stopped in mid-chirp. It was as if the entire universe fell silent at the cries of this child.

Except for Mary, "Oh, let me hold Him," she cried. So, I placed Him in her arms, and she began singing the most beautiful psalm of praise.

About that time Joseph starts banging on the stable door, "What's going on? Is Mary all right?"

"Yes, dear, Mary's fine, the Baby's fine, just let me get them cleaned up before you come in."

I went back and I got them all cleaned up. I asked Mary where the swaddling clothes were, she'd brought for the Baby, but she said, "Oh, let's use some of the ones you brought me." I was so pleased. Wasn't that sweet of her?

I got them all ready, and I went over and opened the door, "All right, Joseph, you may come in now and meet your son."

"Oh, that's not my son," he said as he pushed past me.

Well, I followed closed behind because you can never be sure of what a man's going to do to a baby he knows isn't his, and I was going to make darn sure Joseph didn't hurt either Mary or the Baby. But as it turned out, I needn't have worried. He went over and knelt down next to Mary and he held her so gently and kissed her so tenderly that I knew there was nothing she could ever do that would make him love her less. Then, he looked at that Baby. There came over his face such a look of awe and wonder, that I knew that Baby was safe with him also. No one would ever hurt either one of them as long as Joseph was around.

Mary looked at him and said, "Here, Joseph, you hold Him."

"Oh, no, no, no! I couldn't possibly hold Him."

"Joseph," she said, "You are as important a part of this Child's life as I am. Now, take Him and get to know Him."

Joseph held out his hands, and they were trembling, like most first-time fathers' do. Mary laid the Baby in them and the Baby began to cry. But instead of quickly handing Him back, Joseph pulled Him closer and held Him tighter. He started talking to Him in deep, warm, comforting tones and the Baby quieted right down. We couldn't hear the words, but the tone sounded like he was praying. As we watched, we saw one little tear come out his eye and trickle down his cheek disappearing into his beard.

That's when Simon put his arms around me and whispered in my ear, "Well done, Esther, well done."

I looked up at him through my own tear-filled eyes and said, " You too, Simon, you too."

Now about that time I heard a noise in the stable yard. I went to look and there were all these shepherds standing there, sheep and all. I said, " What do you guys want?"

(*In a deeper voice*) They replied, "We want to see the Baby."

"The Baby? How do you know about the Baby?"

"Well," they said, "We were up there on the mountains when all of a sudden these angels appeared to us and they told us the Son of God had been born down here in Bethlehem and we should come down to see Him, so here we are and we want to see the Baby."

Angels? Yeah, right. Spirits maybe, spirits from a wine sack, but angels? Well, I was about to tell them there was no way I was letting anything that dirty, that smelly, and that bug-infested anywhere near that Baby, and the sheep couldn't come in either, when Mary called to me, "Esther, let them in."

"But Mary... "

"Esther," she said, "Never argue with angels."

To which Simon chimed in, "I've been telling her that for years, but she still argues with me! Ha, ha, ha. Oh, look, hon, even the Baby's laughing."

"That's not laughter, that's gas!"

But we let the shepherds in and there was such oohing and ahhing, over that Baby. Well, I opened up the food basket and started passing it around, and that's when I found out what Simon had meant by "give the children my best." Here he had taken two sacks of our finest wine and had slipped them into the bottom of that food basket. Well, we opened up those wine sacks and started passing them around, and we just had a high old time celebrating the birth of that Baby. But, you know, I never will know how so much wine got in those two little wine sacks.

Sometime in the middle of all this celebrating, Simon and Joseph went out and brought in what they had been working on all this time. Here they had taken an old manger; they had cleaned it out and scrubbed it down. Joseph had made sure there were no splinters or nails or anything sharp that could hurt the Baby. They had filled it with fresh sweet straw, covered it in a thick warm blanket, and, you know, that manger made the perfect bed for that Baby! Is that husband of mine smart, or what? Well after all, he did marry me.

After a while I decided Mary and the Baby had had just about enough excitement for one night, so I started shooing everybody out. Just as Simon and I got to door, Mary called to us. We turned and she said, "God bless you. God bless you both."

We looked at that young family and there was so much love in and around the three of them that you felt you could reach out and touch it. We both said together, " Oh, He has, Mary. He truly has."

Just as we were about to leave, I got hit by a terrible thought. "Mary," I said, "Are you absolutely sure that Baby is who you say He is?"

"Yes, Esther, I'm absolutely sure. Why?"

"Do you mean to tell me I swatted the bottom of the Lord of the universe and made Him cry?"

She laughed, "Under the circumstances, Esther, I think He'll understand."

Well, in the cold morning light, I'm not sure I believe everything that happened in that stable last night, but I know something special did. I intend to keep an eye on that Baby and see what kind of Man He becomes, because if He is who Mary says He is, this world is never going to be the same again. If I were you, I'd get to know the Child and the Man He becomes, because if you do, your lives will never be same again.

(*Looking up as if to the sky*) I think it is just about time that Mary and the Baby are waking up, so I'm going to go and see how they're doing. Oh, I know what you're thinking. Simon laughs at me, too, but he has no room to talk. Do you know what's he's doing today? He's going around the neighborhood trying to drum up business for Joseph. (*In a deep voice*) "Need any carpentry work done? I know a young man, good work, fair prices." But he laughs at me for wanting to help Mary.

"Simon," I tell him, "She is a first-time mother. She is going to need the advice of an older, more experienced woman." And besides, I want to see the Baby!

Well, may God bless you and keep you. May you never get so bogged down in the humdrum problems of day to day living that you fail to see the blessings God showers on you, and may you never grow so old that you do not see with joy and wonder the miracles He continues to perform each and every day.

Amen.

POINTS TO PONDER FOR
THE INNKEEPER'S WIFE

Read Luke 2: 1-20.

1. How does the story of the innkeeper's wife compare to the story you are familiar with hearing?

2. Has this story changed the way you look at the birth of Jesus?

3. Does the more sympathetic view of the innkeeper and his wife conflict with what scripture says?

4. Mary laughs when Esther expresses her desire to know God's plans. Do you think it would be easier to know exactly what God expects of you?

5. In what ways might it make life more difficult?

6. What could have been a reason Hannah and Benjamin had not yet made Esther a grandmother?

7. Has there ever been a situation in your own life where a seemingly unanswered prayer turned out to be a blessing?

8. Do you think Mary's answers to Esther's questions concerning the birth of the Messiah make sense? Why or why not?

9. How do you feel about Mary's answer to Esther's question concerning why God would allow Simon and her to be part of this wondrous event?

10. Have you ever been part of wondrous event, but have felt unworthy?

11. Did Joseph's reaction to the Baby seem plausible?

12. What was it like to be the earthly father of Jesus?

13. What the does story tell you about the relationship between Simon and Esther? Between Joseph and Mary?

14. What does the story tell you about the relationship between God and humankind?

15. In what ways do you think the visit of the shepherds helped Esther to accept what Mary had told her?

16. How do you think all of what happened effected Simon's and Esther's faith?

17. Scripture tells us that Mary "pondered these things in her heart." What do you think that means?

18. What has God done for you that you ponder in your heart?

THE
WOMAN AT THE WELL

John 4: 5-30

Good morning. I am delighted to be here. I am always delighted to come out and tell my story. I am amazed that any of you have ever even heard of me. But I suppose that is because what Jesus did was so (*pause as if searching for the word*) surprising, so unorthodox. Maybe I should begin at the beginning.

It was one of those really hot, dry days. You know the kind: the kind where it feels like the heat is coming right up out of the ground itself, when every time you take a step the dust flies up and gets caught in your mouth and your nose until you feel like you can barely breathe at all. It was one of those days. I was on my way out to Jacob's Well, which is right outside the little village of Sychar, where I live. It was about noon. Now, I know what you're thinking.

You're thinking, "Why don't you go out in the early morning hours, when it's cooler like the rest of the women do."

Well, the truth of the matter is: I don't like being with those other women. You see, they're always talking about me behind my back; making these snide little remarks and these nasty little innuendos and laughing at me. But if I call them on it, they get oh so sweet, butter wouldn't melt in their mouths, "Oh no, dear, we're not talking about you."

Yeah, right. I know they're talking about me, and I know why they're talking about me. I think they're jealous of me. You see, I have no husband and no children. To hear them talk, husbands are more trouble then they're worth, and children can be more of a curse than a blessing.

But if I'm going to be honest with you, and I really should be honest with you, the real reason they talk about me is because I am one of THOSE WOMEN. Yeah, you know the kind: the kind you warn your daughters not to grow up to be.

(*Talking to an invisible child*) "Eat your vegetables, dear; you don't want to grow up like one of THOSE WOMEN."

(*Talking to a bigger invisible child*) "Watch how you dress darling; you don't want people thinking you're one of THOSE WOMEN."

(*Talking to a bigger invisible child*) "Learn to please your husband, sweetheart; you don't want to end up like one of THOSE WOMEN."

Well, I am one of THOSE WOMEN. I'm not really sure how it happened. I mean, I ate my vegetables, and I watched how I dressed. (*Looking off rather dreamingly*) As did a lot of the menfolk. And I learned to please my husband. And a few other women's husbands along the way which I suppose is how I ended up being one of THOSE WOMEN. But be that as it may, I would just as soon come out here in the middle of the hot day and avoid all that hassle.

This particular day, as I approached the well, I was surprised to see this man sitting there. Now, that in itself was unusual because men didn't often come out at this time of day either, and when they did they usually traveled in her... I mean groups, so to see this one lone solitary man sitting there was quite odd.

As I got closer, I realized that this guy was a Jew. I could tell by the way He was dressed. That was really strange, because Jews never, ever come into Samaria. I don't know why. I mean, we come from the same heritage, but something happened years and years and years ago that split our two nations, so Jews don't want to have anything to do with Samaritans and Samaritans don't want to have anything to do with Jews. I know it has something to do with the fact that Jews say you must worship God in the temple in Jerusalem while we Samaritans think it is perfectly all right to worship Him up here on the mountain. Now what I don't understand is: If God is the God of all creation, as we believe Him to be, and God is a Spirit, as we believe Him to be, what difference does it make where we worship Him? Isn't He everywhere?

But every time I ask one of the menfolk this, I get the same answer, "You're a woman; you couldn't possibly understand these things."

I think the truth of the matter is that they don't understand either; they're just not willing to admit it.

As I got even closer, I realized that not only was this guy a Jew, He was a rabbi. I could tell by His prayer shawl. Now I was sure He wasn't going to have anything to do with me, because rabbis don't even talk to their own wives in public, which is something else I don't understand that nobody will explain to me. So, I decided I would just go and get my water. I wouldn't speak to Him. I wouldn't even look at Him.

Actually, I did look at Him. I just wanted to see if He were cute. And He was. He had this head full of curly brown hair, and this nice, full, soft looking brown beard. He had a faraway look in His eyes, as if He were off somewhere in another world. It must have been a very beautiful world because there was a little smile playing around His lips, and He had such a look of peace and joy about Him that there was nothing I wanted more at that particular moment than to be in that world with Him. But I knew that wasn't about to happened, so I just went about getting my water.

The next thing I know I hear Him say, "Would you please give me a drink?"

I looked around, because I figured someone else must have arrived, but there was no one else there. I said, "I'm sorry, but did you say something?"

"Yes," He said, "I asked if you would please give me a drink."

"Why are you, a Jew, asking me, a Samaritan, for a drink of water?"

He said, "Because I'm thirsty."

Now, you really can't argue with that, can you? So, I gave Him the drink and He thanked me. Then

He said something really weird. He said, "If you knew who was asking, you would ask me, and I would give you living water."

I said, "Living water? What do you mean living water?"

He said, "I mean water that can bubble up and wash away all your dirt; water that can renew and refresh in such a way that you will never be thirsty again."

Never be thirsty again? No more having to come out here in the middle of the hot day just to avoid those snide little remarks and those nasty little innuendos? No more having to lug those heavy water jugs all the way back into Sychar? I said, "Well, Sir, that sounds pretty good. Why don't you tell me about this living water?"

He smiled and said, "Why don't you go get your husband and I'll tell you both about it?"

I said, "Oh, I'm not married!"

He said, "I know you're not married. You've already been married five times, and the man you're living with now isn't your husband at all."

Ay Vey! That's torn it. My first thought was that those other women must have told Him about me, but that didn't make any sense. I mean, why would He sit out here all those hours in the hot sun just to condemn me, when they are perfectly capable of doing it themselves? Oh, He was right. I have been married five times. But they weren't all my fault!

My first husband and I got married when we were just too young. Nobody told us how hard marriage is, how much work it involves. We just were not ready for that kind of commitment, that kind of responsibility. So, we went our separate ways. Nobody got hurt.

My second husband was a mama's boy. It was, "Mama always rolled her bread thinner than you do. Mama always wove her cloth tighter than you do. Mama always laid her reeds this way on the floor, not this way on the floor. (*Indicating two different directions*)" It was "Mama this" and "Mama that" and "Mama the other thing" until I finally sent him home to his Mama. I figured we'd all three be happier. And we were.

My third husband and I were getting along just fine, until this woman moved in next door. Now, she was about as smart as a sack of grain, but she was a well filled sack of grain, I can tell you. He started spending more and more time with her, and less and less time with me until finally he didn't come home at all. Well, I figure if he wants the kind of a woman who can't put two words together without one of them being wrong, than more power to him and good luck to them both, because they're going to need it.

My fourth husband tended to hit the wine sacks. After hitting the wine sacks, he started hitting me! Now, I don't care what any holier-than-thou rabbi says, I am not sticking around and let some man beat me to a bloody pulp just because of some stupid vows I may have made. And, if that's what God expects of me, then I don't want to have anything to do with Him either, because it just doesn't make any sense.

My fifth husband wanted to be king of the palace. He wanted his every order obeyed immediately and without question; his every whim satisfied ASAP. Now, I might, might mind you, have been able to deal with that, except he started spending every night out with the boys. The palace becomes a very cold and lonely place when you are there by yourself every night, so I started spending every night out with boys. I figured what's good for the gander is good for the goose, right? Unfortunately, he didn't see it that way. I came home one morning and found all my belongings piled up outside the palace door. I had been banished from the kingdom.

That was all right because one of the boys took me in. He and I have getting along just fine. We've even talked of marriage, but I have had five bad experiences and he hasn't fared much better, so we figure what is the point? I mean, what difference does it make if you stand up in front of some rabbi and your friends and take these vows that you probably have no intention of keeping anyway? And whose business is it anyway? We're not hurting anyone just living together. Why can't they just go away and leave us alone?

But you know, I had the feeling this man wasn't going to accept any of those explanations. I couldn't even look at Him. I just stood there looking down at my feet. I didn't want to see the same look of disgust and condemnation on His face that I see on everyone else's. I know what I am. I know what I've done. I just didn't want Him to know.

I don't know how long we stood there like that. He never said a word. He just waited. Finally, I could stand it no longer and I looked up at Him. But instead of disgust and condemnation, I saw compassion and understanding.

"Naomi," He said, I never will know how He knew my name, "Naomi, for what are you truly thirsting?"

Before I knew what I was saying, I blurted out, "I want to be loved! I want somebody to look at me and not see the woman that I have been but look at me and see the woman that I want to be. Someone that will help me to become that woman. Someone that makes me feel like my life matters to him; that I am the most important person in the whole world to him!"

He smiled at me, "That is exactly the kind of love God is offering you. That's the living water I'm talking about the love of God. Water that can bubble up inside you and wash away all the sins of your past so you need never be bothered by them again. Water that can renew your spirit and refresh your soul so you can go on and be the woman God saw in you when He created you. Water that, because it flows from the very heart of God, it will never run dry and you need never be thirsty again. And Naomi, believe me when I tell you there is no one on earth more important to God than you are."

Now, this was all getting a little too personal for my way of thinking, so I tried to change the subject, "Sir, obviously you are a prophet, so maybe you can explain something to me. Your people say that we must worship God in the Temple in Jerusalem, while my people say it is perfectly all right to worship Him up here on the mountain. Now what I don't understand is: If God is indeed the God of all creation, as we believe Him to be, and God is a spirit, as we believe Him to be, what difference does it make where we worship Him? Isn't it more important HOW we worship Him?"

He broke into a big smile. "Naomi," He said, "You've got it! God is indeed a Spirit, and a spirit cannot be confined to any time or place. It doesn't matter if you worship Him in the Temple or up here on the mountains, for He is indeed everywhere. But God is also the God of truth. When you worship Him, you must worship Him in the spirit of truth. Go before Him. Confess you sins and you will find pardon. Tell Him of your needs and He will meet those needs abundantly. Express your love for Him and He will return that love multifold."

"Well, Sir, I know that the prophets say God will send His Messiah. Is He coming only to you Jews, or will He come for us Samaritans also? I mean, we come from the same heritage. Will the Messiah come for us, or has God truly forsaken us?"

"Oh, Naomi," He said, "God never forsakes His children. The Messiah is coming to Jews, but He is also coming to the Samaritans, and even to the Gentiles, for all are children of the living Lord."

"Sir, you speak with such authority, but how can you be so sure?"

"Because, Naomi, I am the Messiah, and I have come to you."

Whoa! Now that was more than I was bargaining for, but I really wanted to believe Him. Not only because of things He said and the way He said them, but because of His disciples. You see, by this time they had returned from wherever it was they had gone, yet not one of them dared to interrupt us. Not one of them said to me, "Woman, get away from here. Don't bother the master." Not one of them said to Him, "Master, why are you bothering with this woman?" They just stood to the side and let us talk. Now any man who can command that kind of respect from his disciples is someone to whom you should listen.

"Sir," I said, "I would love for my man to hear all of this. If I go and get him, do you promise you will be here when we return?"

"Yes, Naomi, I promise you I shall be here."

So, I ran. I ran all the way back into Sychar, back to my house, but my man wasn't there. I went in search of him and found him in the marketplace, surrounded by a group of his friends talking about whatever it is that men talk about when they get together.

I ran up to him, "You have to come with me."

"Naomi," He said, "What's wrong?"

"I have met the most wonderful man out by the well!"

"Oh, another man. Well, what is he this time, Naomi: blonde, brunette, or redhead?"

"No, you don't understand. It's not like that. This man is a prophet. He has told me everything I have ever done."

"Everything?"

"Yes, everything! And He talks about God in a way I've never heard anyone talk about Him before. Now, we know that God is going to send His Messiah. Do you think this man could be He?"

"Oh right, Naomi, the Messiah of the Lord God Almighty is going to come into Sychar and reveal Himself to you."

"The least you could do is to come and talk with Him."

"Oh, I'll come all right. I'll come and show you exactly what kind of a fraud this 'Messiah' of yours is."

His friends said, "We'll come with you. We'll teach this Jew to come into Samaria making these wild claims!"

Well, I didn't care why they were coming, I merely cared that they were. All the way back to the well, I kept praying that He would still be there.

And He was! As we approached, I could hear Him talking to the men, "No, no, no. Don't you understand? I don't want any food. I don't need any food. I'm not hungry. I am doing my Father's will. That is where I get my nourishment. It was what I was sent to do, and it is what you are going to be sent to do. So, listen and learn."

When we got there, He greeted me like an old friend. I introduced Him to my man and his friends, and He greeted them warmly. Then the questioning began. I'll tell you; they threw every question imaginable at Jesus, but He answered them all with wisdom and with insight. It didn't matter how often the same question was asked, Jesus would answer it patiently, rephrasing it, trying to get them to understand what He meant.

After a while the women came out, dragging the children with them, because they wondered what had happened to all the men. Jesus greeted them warmly. He answered their questions, even the children's questions. You know, He never spoke down to anyone. He simply spoke with them in terms and images they could understand.

The questioning and the answering went on for hours, until the day began to wane. On a whim I asked Jesus if He would like to come to my house for dinner, never dreaming He would accept, but He did! All the way back into Sychar the teaching continued. When we got to my house a true miracle happened. The other women went to their own homes and prepared food and brought it to my house to share, because they knew I would never have enough to feed all these people.

They helped me! For the first time in my life, they helped me! For the first time I felt like I was one of them.

The discussions went on far into the night, until finally exhaustion began taking its toll and people began going home. I asked Jesus if He would like to spend the night with us, knowing He wouldn't because after all, we still weren't married, and He certainly wouldn't approve of that. But He agreed!

Early the next morning, the teaching began once again. That's when talk turned to marriage, which I knew it eventually would. Jesus explained that when two people decide to live together, (*hold up index fingers separately*) they are simply that: two people on two different journeys with two different destinations.

(*Bring index fingers together*) However, when those two people decide to marry, they become one family, on one journey, with one destination.

When you put God in the middle of it, then there are no longer two, but three. No matter how rough the journey may become, one of you is strong enough to help the other two along. No matter how twisty and turning the journey may be, one of you always knows where you are going and can guide the other two. When one of you falls, the others are there to pick you up, to help and to heal, to comfort and encourage, to love and cherish. When the worst happens and one of you dies,(*Put one hand behind your back*) the one that is left isn't truly alone, for the Lord continues on that journey, helping, encouraging, guiding, comforting, loving, until finally that journey ends also, (*bring back the finger and hold them up separately again*) and you stand together once more in the presence of the Living Lord."

My man and I looked at each other, and we knew that was the kind of relationship we wanted. So, we were married. Jesus blessed the union. He even provided wine for the celebration, although I'll never know where He got it! This time we were sure it was going to work, because this time we were going to put God in the middle of it.

All too soon Jesus left Sychar, but He left behind Him a new Spirit. You see, we looked at ourselves differently because we knew that we were still part of the kingdom of heaven. We looked at each differently, too, because we knew that because God had accepted us, we must accept each other. Because God has forgiven us, we must forgive each other. However, the biggest change of all came to me, because you see, I was no longer one of THOSE WOMEN, I had become THAT WOMAN, the one that brought the Messiah to Sychar.

My prayer for you this day is that you, too, find that well of living water. Drink deeply from it. Feel it wash away the sins of your past and know you need never be bothered by them again. Drink daily from it. Let it renew your spirit and refresh your soul, so you can go on and be the person that God saw in you when He created you. Drink fully from it, until you are filled to overflowing so that all may see your joy and want to know it source. Share generously, trusting that because it flows from the very heart of God, it will never run dry, and none need ever be thirsty again.

Amen.

POINTS TO PONDER FOR
THE WOMAN AT THE WELL

Read John 4: 1-25

1. Why was Jesus traveling through Samaria?

2. Why was it unusual for a Jew to go into Samaria?

3. When Jesus offers the woman water, she assumes He is offering physical water. What is He truly offering?

4. She is the first person Jesus tells that He is the Messiah. Why would she believe Him?

5. She had not had a successful marriage despite five attempts. Scripture doesn't tell us why. What are some reasons marriages fail? How can faith help in these situations?

6. Jesus treats the woman with respect despite her less than exemplary life. What does this tell us about God's grace?

7. What does it tell us about how we should treat others who are living less than exemplary lives?

8. John 4: 24 tells us we must worship God in spirit and in truth. What does that mean to you?

9. Read John 4: 31-34. What kind of nourishment do you receive when doing God's work?

10. Read John 4: 35-38. To what harvest is Jesus referring when He says the time is now?

11. Who planted the seeds?

12. In today's society, is the harvest ready?

13. How can you be part of the sowing and the reaping?

14. Jesus stayed in Sychar for two days and many came to believe. Although the woman brought Jesus to Sychar, their faith grew because of what He did. What does this teach us about our role in bringing people to God?

15. How do you feel about the description of marriage in the story?

16. How does your relationship compare to it?

17. What is the difference between Naomi's first five marriages and the sixth one she enters into at the end of the story?

18. Do you think this one will last? Why or why not?

19. In her benediction, Naomi tells us to drink deeply, drink daily, and share generously of the living water. How can you do these things?

20. What effect will it have on your life?

THE HEMORRHAGING WOMAN

Luke 8:43-56

(Have someone read the scripture before beginning.)

I cannot believe that is all that is said about an incident that changed my life. My name is Sarah. That disease cost me everything. It cost me my husband. I couldn't really blame him. I wasn't much of a wife. Sometimes the bleeding was so heavy, the pain so great that I couldn't get out of bed. I couldn't give him children, and every man wants sons. When he left, he at least made sure I had a roof over my head and food to eat. He even visited me at first, but when his new wife began giving him the family, he so desperately wanted his visits became fewer and farther between until... Well, I can't even remember the last time I saw him.

It cost me my livelihood. You see, I was a weaver by trade. I wove beautiful cloth, or so they told me, but since everything I touch was considered unclean,

I couldn't sell any. Sometimes my sister Rachel would take some and sell it without telling anyone from where it had come. I felt guilty about that, but I had to survive, didn't I?

It cost me all of my money. Every time a new miracle cure came along, I would try it, and miracles don't come cheaply. Every time a new miracle worker came to town I would go and see him, and miracle workers aren't cheap either. Nothing ever worked.

It cost me my friends. Oh, they were supportive at first, but as the years went by, they began to look at me with suspicion and condemnation. What had I done, they wondered, that would cause God to punish me like this? What sin had I committed that would make Him forsake me? However, no matter how hard I tried I couldn't think of anything I had ever done that was so bad it warranted this type of punishment.

The funny thing was, I never felt like God had forsaken me. There were nights when I was alone in my bed, when the pain had subsided and I couldn't feel the bleeding, that I would pray to Him. There would come over me such a feeling of peace and comfort that I always believed that someday God would heal me, in His own way, in His own time. But as the years passed I began to believe that His own way would be my death, and I was beginning to look forward to His own time.

Then one day Rachel came running in all excited. "Sarah," she said, "There's a new rabbi in town. You have to come and hear Him speak."

"Oh, Rachel, I don't want to go hear some new rabbi tell me what a great sinner I am and how God is perfectly justified in punishing me this way. You know how I feel about that."

"Oh, but this man's different. He talks about a God of grace and forgiveness. Besides, He's healing people."

"Now I get it. Well, Rachel, I don't have any more money to spend on any more miracle workers."

"But He isn't charging anything."

(*Sarcastically*) "Well then, He must be really good. After all, you get what you pay for."

"Well," she said, "He healed Isaac."

Now Isaac was a man who had been blind from birth. He used to come to the marketplace just to beg. On days when I was feeling better, I would go up and sit with him. Isaac didn't mind. After all, we *were* both on the bottom rung of the social ladder. We would sit and talk about all sorts of things.

I remember him telling me, "You know, Sarah, people think my blindness was caused by some sin I committed, or something my parents did, but I don't believe that. When I sit here and feel the warmth of the sun on my face, it's like God is pouring His love down on me. Every time I hear the clink of a coin in my cup, I know that God has moved someone's heart to provide for me."

Simon was lucky. He didn't see the faces on the people who passed us by. Some of them would look at us like we had no reason to be here or anywhere else. They would pick up their robes and walk way around us so not even the hem of their cloaks would get in the dust by these two beggars. Others would stop and search through their purses for the smallest coin possible and drop it into his cup with great aplomb, and then walk away with a self-satisfied smile because they had helped the poor beggar. But then there were those who would stop and talk with us awhile. They would reach into their purses and drop coins in his cup without ever counting the cost. They would walk away with a smile and a "God bless you." Those people make me believe God really was caring for Isaac.

But Isaac healed?

I said, "Well, I'm glad for Isaac, but this man isn't going to want to help me."

Rachel said, "Oh, you don't know that. The least you could do is ask."

"No, I don't even want to get my hopes up anymore."

"At least go and talk to Isaac. See what he thinks."

"Oh, I don't know," I hesitated.

"Sarah," she said, "what have you got lose?"

She had me there. I didn't have anything to lose. So, I promised her I would at least go and talk to Isaac. I went up to the marketplace, but Isaac wasn't in his usual spot. I looked around, and there he was dancing from stand to stand, picking up things and laughing about how different everything was from what he had imagined, all the while singing the praises of God.

As he danced past me, I called to him, "Isaac, what happened?"

He came back. He looked at me with such puzzlement on his face. He stroked my forehead and my cheeks, and he said, "Sarah?"

I nodded because my throat was closed with emotion.

"Oh, Sarah, you're even more beautiful than I had imagined." (*As an aside*) Well, after all, the man had been blind from birth. Then he grabbed me by the arm, "Sarah, you have to come see Jesus. He can help you; I know He can!"

That's when I got my voice back, "No, Isaac, I'm really happy for you, but this Jesus isn't going want to help me."

"You don't know that."

"Besides, I wouldn't even have the nerve to ask Him."

"Then I'll ask Him for you."

"I don't know..."

"Sarah," he said, "What have you got to lose?"

There it was again. So, I promised Isaac I would think about it, and I did. I thought about all that evening while I picked at my skimpy supper. I thought about it all that night as I lay alone in my bed. Every time I threw an argument out into the darkness as to why I shouldn't go see Jesus; the same answer came back: What have you got to lose?

By morning I had decided I would go and hear Jesus preach. If I liked what I heard, then I would ask if He could help me. I got all covered from head to toe because no one must know what I was up to, and I left to look for Jesus. I no more than shut the door when I realized I didn't have the slightest idea where to find Him. Then I figured that sooner or later, everyone came through the marketplace so I would look for Him there.

When I got there, the marketplace was filled with excitement. I stopped a young boy and asked what was going on.

He said, "Jairus has asked the Master Jesus to come to his house and heal his daughter."

Now, Jairus was the leader of the local synagogue, and he was usually the first one to condemn these traveling rabbis. If he was asking Jesus for help, maybe there really was something to this man.

I was about to ask the boy where I could find Jesus, but he was off and running. I looked across the marketplace, and there was a whole group of people walking with great purpose towards Jairus' house. I figured that Jesus must be one of them, but how would I ever know which one He was?

As it turned out, that was no problem at all. You could tell who was the center of this crowd. Everyone was crowded around Him, hanging on His every word. As they passed, I got in behind Him. I figured if I could just get close enough, I could reach out and touch Him, and if I felt anything, anything at all, then I would ask if He could help me.

I started maneuvering my way behind Jesus. As I got close, I saw Isaac walking next to Him, talking with Him like an old friend. He was telling Jesus about all the things he had seen for the first time, and how different everything was from what he had imagined. They were laughing together about it. Jesus wasn't laughing one of those polite little, "Ha, ha, isn't that nice, why do I always get stuck with the weirdoes" laugh. It was a full, rich, "Isn't that wonderful and isn't God grand!" laugh.

I said a little prayer of thanks for Isaac, because he would keep Jesus busy so He wouldn't know I what I was up to. When I got close enough, I reached out. Just as I was about to touch Jesus, a tassel on His prayer shawl bounce up and touched my hand! (*Pull up and back your hand with a shocked look.*)

I felt like I had been struck by lightening! The pain was gone! The bleeding had stopped! I was healed! I wanted to cry out, "Oh, praise God, I'm whole again!" But I couldn't because no one must ever know what I had done.

I turned and started to go home to thank God in private when suddenly everything stopped, and I heard those three little words that changed my life, "Who touched me?" There was no anger in them, merely curiosity, "Who touched me?"

The anger came from His disciples, "What do you mean, 'Who touched me?' You're surrounded by a mob of people. Anyone could have touched you. How are we supposed to know who it was?"

"No," He said, "Somebody touched me, for I felt the power go out from me." He started looking over the crowd.

My stomach was filled with butterflies. I kept praying, "Oh, dear Lord, please don't let it be me. It can't be me! I didn't even touch Him. I merely touched a tassel on His prayer shawl. How could He possibly know?"

The crowd had grown so quiet you could have heard a feather fall to the ground. He kept turning and turning, coming closer and closer. The butterflies in my stomach flew into my throat and formed a lump. I couldn't speak. I could barely breathe. My heart was pounding so hard I thought it would burst through my chest. Finally, His eyes met mine and He stopped. I knew that He knew that I had been the one who touched Him.

I fell to ground at His feet and started to cry. I wanted to tell Him why I had done what I did, but the words wouldn't come. How could I tell this healthy young man what twelve years of disease and pain can do to you? How could I tell this popular man what twelve years of loneliness and ostracism mean? To never see a welcoming smile or hear a kind word; to never have a handshake of welcome or a helping hand up; to never feel arms around you in comfort or affection. How could I tell this holy man of God that I, a sinful woman, could ever even imagine God would tell me to do this thing? How could I tell Him anything at all, when all I could was lay in the dirt at His feet and cry?

Suddenly, there were hands under my arms lifting me to my feet. I thought they were the hands of the disciples; that they were going to drag me away. I didn't know what would happen to me, and I didn't care. Those few moments of health and wholeness were worth whatever happened now.

But instead of being dragged away, I was pulled closer. They were His hands lifting me up, His arms holding me close: so close I could smell the sweetness of incense on Him, so tight I could hear His heart beating.

My shawl had fallen off of my head, and He was whispering in my ear, "Hush, child, hush."

Child! He was calling me His child. This man, who looked young enough to be my son, if God had granted me one, was calling me His child, and it felt right. I felt like a child again, safe in my father's arms.

"Hush, child, hush," He said, "I understand."

Without a single word, He understood the hope and desperation which had brought me to this moment.

"Hush, child, hush," He said, "I understand. Everything's all right."

He didn't care that I had broken every rule of society by coming to Him. He didn't care that everyone was staring at us. He didn't care that I was making a fool of myself and Him, there in the middle of the marketplace. All that mattered to Him at that moment was me.

I don't know how long we stood like that. Finally, I got control of myself. I pulled back and I looked at His face. And what a wonderful face He had. He was smiling at me: a warm, wonderful, welcoming smile. And His eyes! Oh my, His eyes were so deep and dark I thought I could see the very heavens themselves in them. I saw something else there, too. I saw joy. Joy for me, for Sarah.

Then He said in a voice loud enough for everyone to hear, "Go in peace. Your faith has made you whole."

My faith! In front of all these people who had always told me God had forsaken me, He was praising my faith. My soul soared!

Then a messenger arrived from Jairus' house, "The mistress says not to bother coming. The child has died."

Guilt came crashing down. Jairus' daughter was dead, and I was to blame. If I had not delayed Jesus, He would have arrived in time. I knew it. The whole crowd knew it. The mumbling began.

But Jesus' eyes never left mine, and the smile never left His lips. "No," He said, "the child is not dead, she is merely asleep." Then He nodded at me to make sure I understood what He was saying.

I nodded back, because I believed Him. At that moment I would have believed anything He said. Then He kissed me. Right there in the middle of the marketplace, He kissed me. Right here, (*Pointing to the middle of your forehead*) in the middle of my forehead, He kissed me. Then He turned and left.

The people started to follow Him, some of them congratulating me and others looking at me like I still had no reason for being anywhere. When the last of the crowd had passed, I heard one small voice behind me, "See, I told you, you had nothing to lose!" I turned and there was Rachel. We started laughing and hugging. We went back to my house to thank God for what he done for me and to pray for Jairus' daughter.

It wasn't long before Isaac came around. "The Master was right; the child was merely asleep. She's up now eating lunch with her parents." Then we thanked

God some more for what He had done for Jairus' family.

My life changed after that. Oh, there were still those days when the aches and pains of everyday living began to get to me, but it really didn't matter because I knew God would help me deal with them. And there were those who still treated me as if I was unclean and didn't have a right to be anywhere. They didn't matter either because I knew that God saw and accepted me for who I am. On the days when I began to feel particularly low or sorry for myself, I would remember that day. I would think about how Jesus kissed me, right there in the middle of the marketplace, right here in the middle of my forehead, and the memory of that kiss would warm me all over.

One day, not long thereafter, I was surprised to look out my door and see Jairus' wife and daughter standing there looking very, very lost. Well, after all, they had never been in this neighborhood before. I went out to see if I could help. Imagine my surprise when she asked me if I knew where she could find the woman who had been healed the same day Jesus had saved her daughter.

I said, "I am she," and invited them in. I was even more surprised when they accepted my invitation.

As we shared my meager hospitality, she told me what had happened at her home and asked me about me experience with Jesus. While I was finishing my story she suddenly blurted out, "I understand you're a weaver."

"Yes, yes I am."

She said, "Well, I want to do something to show God how much I appreciate what He did for my family. If I provide you with the raw materials, would you weave cloth, so we can make coats for any child in the village that needs one?"

This was like an answer to prayer for me, because I, too, wanted to do something to show God how much I appreciated what Jesus had done for me, but I lacked the means. I willingly agreed.

Her daughter, Tabitha, or Dorcas if you prefer the Greek, became the go-between. Every time I needed anything, she would bring it to me. Often, she would stay and talk. I taught her how to spin and weave and sew. Between the three of us, we made enough coats so that not only did every child who needed one get it, any widow who was in need received one also.

Tabitha and I became great friends. She was like the daughter I never had, and I became a second mother to her. Despite all of our differences, we found we had much in common. After all, we had both been touched by the Master's hands.

Now, I know what you're thinking. You're thinking, "It's easy for you. After all, you met Him face-to-face." I tell you; you meet Him face-to-face every day. Look at each other. Do you see Him, for He is there? In every smile of welcome, in every word of encouragement, He is there. Reach out and touch someone. (*Make sure everyone is connected to someone*) *Do* you feel Him, for He is there. In every handshake or helping hand up, He is there. In every hug of comfort or affection, He is there.

Indeed, how else can He touch the world, except through *your* hands? How else can His voice be heard, except through yours? How else can His love be known, except through you?

So, go forth from this place knowing that you have been touched by the Master's hand, and take that knowledge with you. Let God use you so that all you meet may know they, too, have been touched by the Master's hand.

Amen.

POINTS TO PONDER FOR
THE HEMORRHAGING WOMAN

Read Luke 8: 43-55

1. In this story, how was Sarah's life impacted by her disease?

2. What challenges have you faced because of things over which you have no control?

3. Sarah's friends seem to blame her for what has happened. Have you ever felt you have been unfairly blamed for something over which you have no control?

4. Did you feel that God was with you even when your friends weren't?

5. Isaac feels God provides for him despite his difficult circumstances. When have you felt God was near in difficult times?

6. Sarah wants to know more about Jesus before asking for help. Have you ever been reluctant to go to Jesus for help?

7. What were the reasons for your hesitation? Were they valid?

8. Although Sarah never asks Jesus for help, she is still healed. In what ways did she go to God for help? How do you seek God's help?

9. While Jesus was dealing with Sarah, a messenger arrives to tell Him not to come because Jairus' daughter had died. Has there ever been a time when you felt Jesus shouldn't be bothered because there is nothing He can do?

10. Read Luke 8: 51-55. Jesus had just performed a healing witnessed by a great crowd. Why would He only allow Peter, James, John, and the girl's parents to see Him raise her?

11. Why were they told not to tell anyone?

12. Sarah tells us there were still people who wouldn't believe she was healed. Have you ever experienced a time when people doubted your relationship with God? How did you react to them?

13. Although it is not scriptural, according to this story how did Jairus' wife show her gratitude to God?

14. Why would she have sought out Sarah's help?

15. Sarah and Tabitha became great friends. What were some of things that bound them together?

16. Think of someone who has faced similar challenges to yours. How have your common struggles brought you together?

17. How have they helped in facing those challenges?

18. How can you be the hands and feet of God in this world so others may be touched by the Master's hand?

THE
CANAANITE WOMAN

Matt. 15: 21-28

Good morning. My name is Jael, and I am a
Canaanite woman. Now I know that conjures up all
sorts of images for you. The Canaanites, worshippers
of Baal and myriad other minor gods and goddesses.
The Canaanites, livers of immoral lifestyles. Well, you
know, you really shouldn't judge people by labels. Not
all of us Canaanites worship Baal or any of the minor
gods, and we don't all live immoral lifestyles.

It's like if I were to say, "Roman soldier," you'd
probably get the picture of a big burly man who thinks
that might makes right. Someone who thinks that
because he is so big and burly, he can take whatever he
wants, whenever he wants from whomever he wants.
But not all Roman soldiers are like that either. The
centurion who commands the men in our sector takes
Pax Romano, the peace of Rome, very seriously. He
keeps a close eye on his men to make sure they are not
exploiting the very people they are there to protect.

And then there are Jews. Yahweh's chosen people, who feel that because they are the chosen ones, they can look down their noses at the rest of us and not treat us with any kind of respect or consideration at all. But not all Jews are like that either. Some Jews see being one of Yahweh's chosen not so much as a place of privilege, but rather as one of responsibility.

My friend Rebecca is like that. She owns the stand in the marketplace next to mine. You see, when my husband died, I needed to find some way of supporting my daughter Jazrel and me. Everyone always told me I made such beautiful pottery, so I decided to go into the pottery business. I was a bit hesitant about taking the stand because of the Jew next door, but Rebecca turned out to be just the nicest person. We got to be very good friends. We can talk about anything.

Rebecca hasn't had a very easy life either. She had been married to a very abusive husband. While she was carrying their child, he beat her so badly that she lost the babe. Then he threw her out. She might have died, but two other Jewish women took her in and nursed her back to health. Now the three of them weave cloth and make clothing that Rebecca sells at the stand. Yet with as hard as her life has been, there is a peace and joy about her that I truly envy. She says it comes from Yahweh. I don't know. I've never put much stock in any of these gods, but, hey, whatever works for you, right?

One day I was working on a small idol for a customer of mine and we started talking about it. I explained that when a person can't afford an idol of gold or silver, they'll come to me and I'll make the one.

Rebecca asked, "How do you know what it's supposed to look like?"

"Well, usually the customer tells me what they want, and I'll do a rough sketch and work from that."

"Well, excuse me for saying so," she said, "but that has got to be one of the ugliest things I have ever seen."

"Isn't it though? Look at the mouth on this thing. The woman wants it for her mother-in-law. I think she's trying to send a message!"

"Of what is it supposed to be a god?"

"I don't know. What does it matter? To me, it's a god of nothing."

"You don't believe in them?"

"No, how can I? Look at this: it's made of clay, basically dirt and water. I can make it look like anything I want. I can crush it in one hand if I choose. Even after the hardening process, I could break it into a thousand pieces and the 'god' can't do anything to stop me. Yet, someone is going to take this home. They'll put it in a place of prominence, probably have to nail it down to keep it from getting accidently knocked over, and then they'll bow down and worship it. Yet, if the house catches on fire, they're going to have to rescue the god instead of the other way around. What I have never been able to figure out is when does the spark of divinity enter into this thing? I mean, how can anything I create be greater than me the creator?"

"What about Baal? "

"Baal is nothing more than a giant idol; designed by men, created by artisans, and worshipped by fools. He has no eyes to see, no ears to hear, no hands to help and no heart to love. No, if I ever find a god worthy of worship, he'll be greater than I am. He'll see me in every situation. He'll hear me when I cry out to him. He'll be powerful enough to help me, but above all, he'll have a heart to love me. If I ever find a god like that, him I could truly worship.

"What about this Yahweh of yours? Who created Him?"

"Oh no one created Yahweh, " she said, "Yahweh always has been and always will be. Rather, Yahweh created everything."

"What does He look like?"

"No one has ever seen Yahweh."

"No, I mean what does the statute of Him look like in the temple where you worship?"

She said, "There are no statutes of Yahweh. Yahweh strictly forbids the making of graven images."

"Well then, how do you know what He's like?"

"Well, Yahweh puts an aspect of Himself in everything He creates. Since Yahweh created everything, all you have to do is look around and you can see what He's like."

I said, "I'm sorry, Rebecca, but I haven't got the slightest idea what you're talking about."

"Look at the mountains. See how grand they are? Their grandeur is the grandeur of Yahweh. You remember the storm we had two nights ago; how powerful it was? That power is the power of Yahweh. You know how beautiful a field of lilies look when they are in full bloom? Their beauty is the beauty of Yahweh. And if you stand outside on a starlit night and look up into the heavens, they seem to go on and on, stars twinkling as far as the eye can see. That vastness is the vastness of Yahweh, and the stars are there to remind us that not even the blackest of nights can ever extinguish the light of Yahweh."

"So, Yahweh created everything and puts an aspect of Himself in everything He creates."

"That's right."

I thought about and said, "What about bugs? How are they an aspect of Yahweh?"

She laughed a little, "You know, I have never heard anyone address that, and if you ever tell anyone I said this, I'll probably deny it, but to me, bugs are the persistence of Yahweh."

I said, "What?"

"Yes," she said. "Think about it. No matter how hard you try you can never completely get rid of bugs. They are always there. Even if you try to ignore them, they will remind you of their presence with little nips and itches, spider webs, something. Well, that's the way it is with Yahweh. No matter how hard you try, you can never completely get rid of Yahweh. He is always there. Even if you choose to ignore Him, He will remind you of His presence with little nips of conscience. Ergo, bugs are the persistence of Yahweh."

You know, I have never been able to look at bugs the same way since!

I thought about it some more and said, "What about people? Did Yahweh create all people or just you Jews?"

"Oh no," she said, "Yahweh created everyone."

"But Rebecca, look around you. We are all so different: different sizes, different shapes, different colors, different genders. How is THAT aspect of Yahweh?"

She said, "That is the diversity of Yahweh."

"But, Rebecca, you and I both know that there are some awfully nasty people out there. People that would just as soon kill you as look you. People that will lie and cheat and steal simply because they can. Now how are THEY an aspect of Yahweh?"

"That is the freedom of Yahweh. You see, Jael, of all the creatures Yahweh created, human beings are the only ones to whom He gave freedom of choice. Animals behave out of instinct. A lion kills because it must. A bird flies because it knows no other. Only human beings can choose to be kind or cruel, to help or to hurt, to love or hate, to forgive or carry a grudge. Why, you can even choose to accept Yahweh or reject Him. That is the freedom of Yahweh."

"But if Yahweh created everyone, why does He destroy so much of His creation? I mean, He practically annihilated my people to give your people our land. To say nothing of what He did to the Egyptians, the Amelekites, the Philistines, and the Babylonians. Why would He destroy so much?"

"You know, Jael, your pottery is exquisite."

I thought she was trying to change the subject! "Well, thank you, but... "

"No, hear me out. Does every piece you make turn out this beautifully?"

"No, this represents my finest work."

"What happens when a piece doesn't turn out the way you want?"

"Well, if it's early in the process, I'll work with it. I'll add clay or take away clay, shape it, reshape it trying to get it to be what I want it to be. Sometimes I have to start all over again. If it is after the hardening process, and it still isn't what I want, I'll smash it."

"Why?"

"Because this pottery reflects on me the potter and I only those pieces that reflect positively on me."

She said, "That's the way it is with Yahweh. Yahweh works hard with His creation, shaping it, reshaping it, trying to get to be what He wants it to be. But sometimes He can do no more with it, and then He'll destroy it.

"But that sounds so cruel."

"Jael," she said, "I know how much your pottery means to you. I have seen the pride on your face when somebody praises you for it. I've seen the joy you share with a young bride as she buys the first piece for her new home. I have even seen you slip extra pieces into an order even though you know she can't afford it simply because it gives you pleasure to give. Now how do you feel when you have to destroy something on which you've worked so hard?"

I thought about it, and said, "*To* tell you the truth, Rebecca, there have been times when I have worked so hard on a piece, put so much of myself into it but it still hasn't come out right and I've had to destroy it, that I've wept."

She said, "That's the way it is with Yahweh. Yahweh loves His creation. He takes pride in it whenever anyone praises Him for it. He will share graciously and generously. So, when He has to destroy something, He weeps."

A God who is that involved with His creation? A God who takes pride in it, who wants to share it? And a God who weeps if He has to destroy it?

I thought about it some more. "But what about you Jews? You are Yahweh's chosen people, but He has not always treated you kindly. I know about the years of slavery in Egypt, the 40 years of wandering in the wilderness, to say nothing of the Babylonian Exile. Why would He treat His own people so harshly?"

Rebecca said, "Jael, Jazrel is a wonderful young girl."

I thought she was trying to change the subject again. "Well, thank you, but. . ."

"No, just listen. She is so polite, so obedient, so hard working, is she always this good?'

I just snorted, "No, she is not always this good. We have some battle royals over her behavior, I can tell you."

"Why do you bother?"

"Because she is my daughter and I love her. I want her to be the very best person she can be, and I don't want her to ever bring shame to her father's name."

"That's the way it is with Yahweh. You see, Jael, being one of Yahweh's chosen doesn't mean more privileges, it means we have more responsibilities because Yahweh has told us what He expects of us through the Law and through the prophets. So when we are not the people Yahweh wants us to be, He disciplines us, not out of anger, but out of love, because He wants us to be the very best people we can be and He doesn't want us to ever bring shame to our Father's name, to His name."

A God who disciplines not out of anger, but out of love? A God who wants only the best for His people? Now this is God I truly wanted to know about.

I wasn't really sure how to go about it, so that night after I got Jazrel to sleep, I simply began talking to Him.

(*Looking up*) "Yahweh, are You really in the grandeur of the mountains?"

(*In a deeper voice*) "I AM.»

(*With a startled look, and glancing up*) Well now, that was a little weird, so I thought I'd try it again. "Yahweh, are You truly in the power of the storm?"

(*In a deeper voice with slightly different emphasis*) "I AM."

Now I was beginning to think I was going a little crazy, and the house was beginning to feel very, very small, so I stepped outside, (*again looking up*) Yahweh, if I were able to travel to the ends of the universe, past that furthest star, would You still be there?"

(*Again, in the deeper voice with another slightly different emphasis*) "I AM."

"Yahweh, are You really answering the cries of this Canaanite woman? This child who wants so desperately to believe in someone greater than she is? Someone who cares about her? Someone who sees her life as important? Someone who thinks her life matters? Yahweh, are You truly seeking me as urgently as I am seeking You?"

(*Pause briefly and then in a tender voice*) "I AM."

This whole thing left me a little shaken, so the next day I went back to Rebecca.

"Rebecca, how does Yahweh speak to you?"

"Well, Yahweh speaks through the Law and through the prophets."

"Oh yeah, I've heard the men in your synagogue arguing about exactly what Yahweh says through the law and through the prophets."

She chuckled a little, "Yes, it's true. Sometimes Yahweh doesn't speak as plainly as we might like, or maybe we don't listen as closely as Yahweh would like."

"How else does He speak to you?"

"Sometimes Yahweh speaks through other people, just like I'm speaking to you now."

"Do you ever actually hear His voice?"

"Oh, yes. In moments of great joy, if you listen you can hear Him laughing. In times of great sorrow, or pain, or challenge, when you cry out to Him, if you listen, you can hear Him say, 'Do not be afraid. I am here, and I am able.' But mostly it's just a feeling we get of His Spirit with us."

"I'm sorry, Rebecca, but I don't know what you mean."

"Well," she said, "hasn't there ever been a time in your life when you have felt someone is with you, even though you know he can't be?"

I thought about it, and, you know, there are times when a man will walk past my stand with that same sweaty earthy smell my husband used to have, and I will feel him with me once more. Times when I have made his favorite meal and with that first savory bite, I can almost taste his pleasure. Times when I will see his smile in Jazrel's and hear his laugh in hers. And there are those times when I am all alone in our bed, missing him so badly that I can almost feel his arms around me and his broad shoulders absorbing my tears as they once did.

Rebecca interrupted my musings, "You're feeling someone right now, aren't you?"

"Hmm, hm."

"That's the way it is with Yahweh. We feel His Spirit and know the peace and comfort which He brings."

Now I wanted to learn more about Yahweh. That's when great excitement came to our village; excitement by the name of Jesus. Oh, the rumors about Him were spreading like wildfire: how He was healing the sick, giving sight to the blind, driving out demons, and speaking the gospel in a way that upset quite a few of the men in the local synagogue.

Then one day Cyrus, a man who had been lame from birth, who used to be brought to marketplace simply to beg, was there dancing, literally dancing, around the marketplace and singing the praises of Yahweh.

As he danced past my stand I cried, "Cyrus, what happened? "

He came dancing back, "Oh, Jael, isn't it wonderful? Look at me! I can dance! (*doing a little dance*) I can leap! (*jump a little*) Jesus has made me whole!"

"But, Cyrus," I cried, "You're not Jewish!"

"He never even asked. He merely asked if I believed He could do, and I did, and He did, and look: I can walk, I can work, I have a life! Oh, praise Yahweh, Jesus has given me life!" And off he danced.

I looked at Rebecca, and she was laughing, " But, Rebecca, he isn't Jewish!"

"I told you, Jael. Yahweh is not just the God of Jews; He is the God of everyone."

"Well, I know that your prophets say Yahweh will send His Messiah. Do you think this Jesus could be He?"

"I'll tell you; the prophets say the Messiah will heal the sick, give sight to the blind, cause the lame to dance, and speak the gospel to all people. Now this Jesus seems to be doing all of that."

"So, you're saying He is messiah?"

"I'm saying if He isn't, He's the closest thing we've seen to him yet."

Now I wanted to hear Jesus preach, but that's when great tragedy struck. My precious little Jazrel became very, very ill. I brought in the wise woman of the village, the one versed in the use of herbs and incantations for healing. She examined Jazrel, but she just shook her head. "The child is possessed by a powerful demon. You might as well prepare a place for her next to her father."

"Oh no! Not my precious little Jazrel. (*looking up*) *Oh* Yahweh, please, she is only eight years old. She has her whole life ahead of her, and she is the only thing I have of value in this whole world. Yahweh, I know You are more powerful than any demon. You can save her. Please, Yahweh, I beg you, save my little girl. Yahweh, are you listening? Yahweh, are You there?"

At that moment the door opened, and Rebecca walked in. "When you weren't at your stand I was afraid something had happened. What's wrong?"

"Oh, Rebecca, Jazrel is ill. The wise woman says she is possessed, and the demon will take her life. Oh Rebecca, I know that Yahweh is more powerful than this or any demon. He could save her. Please, you pray to Him. He'll listen to you."

Rebecca looked at me and said, "You must go find Jesus. Right now, He is at the home of Joseph resting. Go to Him. Don't let anyone stand in your way, not even His disciples. As you approach, call Him son of David, so He knows you recognize His authority. Hurry, He can help you."

I said, "I know He can help me, but are you sure He will?"

She replied, "I am."

Sometimes Yahweh speaks through other people.

I left Jazrel in Rebecca's care while I went in search of Jesus. He was still at the house of Joseph, sitting under a tree resting. There was a loaf of bread and a bunch of grapes in His lap, but He wasn't touching them, He was simply listening to the conversations of His men.

I approached, "Jesus, son of David."

Instantly the disciples were up forming a protective shield around Him, (*In a deeper voice*) "Get away from here, woman. Can't you see the Master's resting?"

Don't let anyone stand in your way, not even His disciples. "Jesus, son of David, please."

(*Again, in a deeper voice*)"We told you to leave the Master alone. He hasn't got time for the likes of you!»

"Jesus, son of David, please, I need your help."

With that His voice rose above those of His disciples, "Sit. Down."

They all went back to their seats mumbling and grumbling and looking at me with such disgust on their faces. When I looked at Jesus, that same look of disgust was on His face, and it frightened me, until I realized He wasn't looking at me, He was looking at them.

When His eyes met mine, the look turned to one of curiosity, "What do you want of me?"

I fell to ground at His feet, "Please, Sir, my little girl is ill. The wise woman says she is possessed, and the demon will take her life. Sir, she is only eight years old. She has her whole life ahead of her. And she is the only thing I treasure in this whole world. Sir, I know

You are more powerful than this or any demon. You can save her. I beg you, Sir, please save my little girl!"

(*In a deeper voice*) "Yeah, right, like He's going to waste His power on the likes of her!"

Again, the look of disgust came over Jesus' face, but again it was directed at the disciples, not at me. When His eyes met mine again, there was twinkle in them, and I could almost hear Him telling me, "Play along with me, they need to learn a lesson."

He said, "I come for the children of Israel. Is it right to give the bread of the children to the dogs under the table?"

(*Deeper voice*)"Oh ho, that's telling her. Canaanite dog thinks she's going to get something from our Lord."

"Please, Sir, I know I am nothing more than a dog, but didn't Yahweh create the dogs as well as the children? Doesn't Yahweh care for the dogs as well as the children? Can't the dogs even get the crumbs the children brush from the table? That's all I'm asking for, Sir, one tiny crumb the children reject to save my little pup."

Suddenly, His face was filled with admiration. "Truly I tell you, I wish the children appreciated the bread as much as you do. But I do not see a dog before me. I see a child of Yahweh, hurting and hungry, seeking help at my Father's table. She will be satisfied. Your daughter is healed." Then He smiled, "But she will be hungry. So here, take this bread and these grapes and when you share them, remember me, and give thanks to Yahweh for all He does through me."

As I reached for the bread and grapes our hands touched, and I felt a surge of power through me, and I knew Jazrel had been healed. I kissed His hands, "Oh thank you, Jesus, Son of David, Son of Yahweh."

He leaned forward and whispered in my ear, "I AM."

I took the bread and grapes, and as I left amid the deafening silence of the disciples, I heard Jesus laughing. I would have loved to stay to hear what He said to the disciples, but I wanted to get home to Jazrel. When I walked in, there she and Rebecca were clapping their hands and singing a psalm of praise to Yahweh.

Jazrel ran to me, "Mommy, mommy, I'm hungry, I'm hungry!"

"Are you, baby? How do you feel?"

"I feel fine, but I'm hungry!"

"Well, it just so happens that the man who saved you knew you would be, so He sent this bread and these grapes. So, let us share, and let us give thanks to Yahweh for all He does through Jesus."

I never made another idol after that. Somehow it seemed like an affront to Yahweh. And I started giving away 20% of all I earned: 10% to the local synagogue and 10% to people like Cyrus had been who I knew needed help.

Then one day Jesus was back in our village, going through the marketplace surrounded by a mob of people. I started calling to Him, "Jesus, over here. Jesus, Son of David, over here!"

He turned, and when He saw me, He broke into a big smile, "Jael!" He fought His way over to my stand. "Jael, how are you?"

"I'm fine, Sir."

"I understand you're giving away 20% of all you earn. You know, you really don't have to, Yahweh only requests 10."

"I know that, Sir. I do not give because I have to; I give because I want to, and because I am able. I want you to meet my daughter. Jazrel, come here. Jesus, this is my daughter Jazrel. Jazrel, this is Jesus, the man who saved you. Look at Him, because when you see Jesus, you see the heart of Yahweh."

There was a momentary look of surprise on His face, followed by one of great pride, not so much in Himself, but in me; as if I had discovered a wonderful secret. "Jazrel, go get the gift we made for Him. (*pause*) Jesus, I cannot eat bread or grapes or even drink wine without remembering You and thanking Yahweh for all You did for us. So, we made you this cup. Rebecca told us what it should look like. We want You to have it so that whenever You drink from it, you will remember these two Canaanite children who are so very thankful they are welcome at Your Father's table."

As He took the cup, He thanked me and got a faraway look in His eyes, "Truly I tell you, when I drink from this cup, I shall remember all of the children my Father invites to the table, but above them all, I shall remember the two of you."

Then He gave us each a hug and a kiss, and He gave Rebecca a hug and a kiss, and He was gone. We never saw Him again after that. We heard rumors that He had been crucified, and they upset me, until Rebecca explained that even that had been prophesized about the Messiah, and we should just wait to see what happens.

Sure enough, a few days later the rumors were flying that He had been seen alive and well and walking around Jerusalem. That set off a fire storm of controversy in the local synagogue. Was He Messiah, or wasn't He? How can any man be fully human and fully God?

Now, I don't understand all the theological aspects of it, I just know what He said to me when I called Him Son of David, Son of Yahweh. He replied, "I AM." That's good enough for me.

My prayer for you this day is that you, too, see Yahweh in all His creation. May you see His grandeur in the mountains, His power in the storms, His beauty in the lilies and, yes, even His persistence in the bugs.

Get to know Jesus, because in knowing Him, you truly do know the heart of Yahweh.

May you feel His Spirit with you. In times of great joy, listen for His laughter. In times of great sorrow, or pain, or challenge, know that He is there, and He is able.

Seek Him with confidence that when you cry out to Him, "Yahweh, are you listening? Yahweh, are you there?" He will reply with His name and His nature, "I AM."

Amen.

POINTS TO PONDER FOR
THE CANAANITE WOMAN

Read Matt. 21-28

1. Jael doesn't believe in any of the gods she has heard about before she learns of Yahweh from her friend Rebecca. What is it about the idols she finds difficult to worship?

2. What are some of the gods people worship in today's world?

3. How does Yahweh differ from these false gods?

4. Rebecca tells Jael that Yahweh puts an aspect of Himself in everything He creates? Do you agree with that? Name something in which you see Yahweh.

5. People sometimes have trouble seeing Yahweh in terrible situations. How can we see Him in the natural disasters? In tragic news stories? In personal failures?

6. When Jael first starts seeking Yahweh, she is surprised and a little frightened at what happens. Has an encounter with Yahweh ever surprised or frightened you?

7. Jael is surprised when Jesus heals Cyrus, because Cyrus isn't Jewish. Do we sometimes believe that Yahweh is only the God of those who believe in Him?

8. What difference does it make to know God is the God of all people?

9. When she goes to Jesus for help, the disciples try to stop her. Have you ever encountered someone who is a stumbling block to others while seeking Yahweh?

10. Have you ever been a stumbling block for someone?

11. Jesus uses the healing of Jael's daughter to teach His disciples that He came for everyone. Did they learn the lesson?

12. How did it change their opinions of outsiders?

13. Jael refuses to make idols after meeting Jesus. How has meeting Him changed your way of life?

14. Is there some behavior you have given up because of Him?

15. In Exodus 3: 14 God tells Moses His name is " I AM." What does that mean to you?

16. What does it mean to know that when Jesus drank from the cup and went to cross, He was thinking of you?

THE
SINFUL WOMAN

John 8: 3-11; Luke 7: 36-47

Good morning. My name is Miriam, and I am a woman who has literally lived two lives. My first life wasn't particularly pleasant. I came from a very large, very poor family. Mom and Dad tried hard to provide for us, but there never seemed to be enough food, enough clothing, enough time, or enough love. As soon as my brothers were able, they were expected to go out and find any little job they could to help my father. My sisters and I were expected to help out around the house. Mom taught us how to weave and sew; what foods could or could not be eaten according the Law and how they had to be prepared. My sisters and I ended up doing most of the work because Mom was always tired, probably because she was always either pregnant or recovering from having a baby. Many of my brothers and sisters never made it past their first birthdays.

Because of the constant childbearing, Mom died very young. As the oldest, I was expected to take over all her duties. I didn't really mind. I enjoyed taking care of my father and my brothers and sisters. Still, I couldn't help but dream of the time when I would have my own home, my own family, and my own children. I promised myself that no matter what they would always know that they were wanted, and cherished, and loved.

After Mom died, Dad started finding his solace in wine sacks. We learned very early on that when Dad started drinking, we made ourselves scarce. You see, Dad was a mean drunk. The slightest noise to disturb him brought his foot to our backsides. The slightest word deemed to be disrespectful brought his hand across our faces. Everyone always told me that I looked like my mother, and in his drunkenness, I must have looked like her to him also, because he would grab me and try things I knew no man should ever try with his daughter. Fortunately, in his drunken state I was able to escape.

And escape I did! Straight to the marketplace. I loved going to the marketplace. I loved everything about it: the crowds of people noisily going about their business, the sounds of haggling, the smell of the animals mingled with that of freshly baked bread. However, my favorite stand of all was the one with the fabrics. Oh, how I loved the fabrics, so different from the coarse homespun I wore. Some of them were so light and sheer that the slightest breeze sent them waving. And the colors! Oh my, they were dyed in every color, shade and tint imaginable. I often thought that if I could ever own a dress made from all those colors that I would feel like an angel dancing through a rainbow! But of course, I knew I would never be able to afford such a dress. Still, a girl can dream. That was the best part of the marketplace: It was filled with dreams and dreams were free.

One day, as I was wandering around, I noticed this man following me. He frightened me at first, because Mom had warned us about such men. Then I recognized him as Simon the Pharisee. Now, Simon was a highly respected man. Simon, it is said, knew the Law forward and backwards and inside and out. If you ever had a question, Simon could answer it. If you ever needed a loophole, Simon would find it. Simon was noted for his long and pious prayers. He could spend hours just praising God for being as great as He is and thanking God for making Simon as great as he is. I often wondered if God ever stopped listening. Simon was a stickler about tithing because "that's what the Law says". Simon, it is said, would tithe down to his last rosemary sprig, his last sesame seed, and was very hard on those of us who had nothing with which to tithe. I never understood what God needed with rosemary sprigs and sesame seeds, but that is not the kind of question one asks. Well, I figured that Simon was following me to make sure I wasn't stealing anything. I knew better than that. My parents taught us the Law, and I knew God hates a thief.

Then one day while I was watching some little lambs play, oh they were so cute, so innocent, so blissfully unaware of what the future held, Simon came and stood beside me. He was eating some freshly baked bread, and my, it did smell good. He offered me some, but I said, "No thank you, Simon."

"Oh, please," he said, " I find I have bought too much. If you don't take it, I'll simply have to throw it to these little lambs, and I would much rather see you have it."

Well, if the truth be known, I would much rather see me have it, too. So, I accepted. It did taste awfully good.

Simon said, "I see you come here often, but you never seem to buy much."

"No, my family doesn't have very much. I just like to come and look at all the things."

"What's your name?"

"Miriam."

"Ah, Miriam: Named after our ancestress, the first prophetess of Israel, sister to our leader Moses. Well, Miriam, I would like to buy bread for your entire family."

"Oh no, Simon, I couldn't let you do that."

"Oh please, the Lord tells us that we should help provide for those less fortunate, so it would be like an offering to God. Surely, you would not deny me the pleasure of giving an offering to God, would you?"

Well, when he put it like that, it almost seemed selfish not to accept. So, I agreed.

That night, my brothers and sisters were so excited. However, Dad was a bit suspicious. "Where'd you get this bread, girl? You didn't steal it, did you?"

"No, Dad, I didn't steal it. Simon the Pharisee gave it to me."

"Simon? Now why would Simon be giving you bread?"

"He said that the Lord wants him to help those less fortunate. He said it was like an offering to God."

"Humph. That doesn't sound like Simon. You be careful, girl," and he went back to his wine sacks, but he ate the biggest chunk of bread.

The next day, I went back to the marketplace hoping to see Simon so I could thank him and tell him how very much my family had appreciated the bread. Yet, I had no idea where to find him. Then, there he was, and it almost seemed as if he were looking for me. But that can't be right. Surely a man like Simon has more important things on his mind than a girl like me.

I ran up to him and I thanked him for the bread and told him how much my family had enjoyed it. He just started grinning. I thought, "What a nice smile he has."

Then he said, "Well, Miriam, I'm glad I found you. I have just sacrificed today and there is so much meat left over, that I want you to have it."

"Oh no, Simon, I couldn't possibly accept meat."

"Oh please," he said, "If you don't take it, it will just spoil. Now surely you wouldn't want to see a sacrifice to God spoil, would you?"

Well, when he put it like that, it almost seemed sacrilegious to refuse. So, I accepted.

That night, our house smelled better than it had in years. My brothers and sisters were so excited. But Dad was even more suspicious, "Where'd you get this meat, girl?"

"Simon gave it to me."

"Why would Simon be giving you meat?".

"Well, he said it was left over from a sacrifice and he didn't want to see it spoil."

"Humph, that doesn't sound like Simon. You be careful, girl," and he went back to his wine sacks, but he also ate the biggest portion of meat.

The next day I went back to the marketplace once again hoping I'd see Simon to tell him how much my family had enjoyed the meat. Sure enough, there he was, and again it looked as if he were looking for me. But that can't be right. I mean, what possible interest would a man like Simon have in a girl like me?

I ran up to him, and I thanked him for the meat, and he just beamed. I thought once again, "What a nice smile he has."

Then he said, "Miriam, what is your favorite thing in the whole marketplace?"

Without hesitation I cried, "Oh, the fabrics!" I took him to the stand and I showed him the fabrics that were so light and sheer that the slightest breeze sent them waving. I told him how I thought if I could ever own a dress made with all those colors, I would feel like an angel dancing through a rainbow.

His eyes lit up, "Oh, Miriam, what a beautiful image! Oh, I must buy you that fabric. I must see what an angel looks like when she's dancing through a rainbow."

I said, "Oh no, Simon, I couldn't let you do that. Why, my sisters would be jealous."

His face fell, "Ah yes, wise Miriam, as wise as your namesake." Then he brightened, "I know, I'll buy you the fabric and we can take it back to my house and you can wear it for me there."

Now my little red warning flags were beginning to fly. "Oh no, Simon, I couldn't let you do that. Why, somebody might see. There might be talk."

"Nobody will see, Miriam. My house is set far back from the road, very secluded and private. And what talk could there be? After all, I'm a Pharisee."

Well, the fabric was so beautiful, and I knew I would never have another opportunity to own such a dress. And after all, he is a Pharisee, and a Pharisee would never do anything wrong, right? So, I agreed.

Simon bought the fabric and we took it to his house. Simon was right, his house set far back from the road, very secluded and private. While I was fashioning a dress, he ordered a meal prepared for us. When I came out, his whole face lit up. He said, "Now, dance for me, Miriam. Dance like our ancestress danced on the day the Lord God Almighty closed the waters of Red Sea over pharaoh's army, washing away chariots and all. Dance, my little angel, dance!"

And I danced my best for him. He clapped and he cheered. I was so glad that I could bring him a little of the happiness he had given my family.

When I was finished, he led me over and sat me down on the softest cushion I had ever felt in my whole life. Then, he fed me the most delicious food I had ever tasted in my whole life.

Then, he offered me wine, but I said, "No thank you, Simon. I would much prefer water. I know what wine does to my father."

"That's because your father doesn't know how to drink it. Wine is truly a gift from God. It warms you from the inside out, just like His love. Here, I'll water it down for you. "

He poured more liquid into the cup. Then he held it to my lips. I took a swallow. It burned going down, but after a moment I knew what he meant. I was beginning to feel warm all over. He gave me another sip, and I began to feel hot all over. Another sip and the room felt as if it were beginning to spin. Then, I didn't feel anything at all.

Until I felt Simon's hand on me, groping up under my dress, going places I knew only a husband had a right to go. I tried to stop him. "No, Simon, please don't."

He slapped me hard across the face. "Shut up! I have invested enough in you. Now it is time for a return on my investment."

I tried to fight him, but he was just too strong. No matter how much I pleaded and cried, he just kept going and going. When he was finished, he leaned back with a self-satisfied smirk on his face. "Now, then, that wasn't so bad was it?"

(*sobbing while talking*) "Yes, yes, it was awful! "

"Oh, quite your bellyaching. You know you wanted it."

"NO, no I didn't!"

"Yes, you did. Girls like you are all alike. You tempt a man past anything he can stand, and then if he acts on it you cry rape. Well, it won't work, Miriam. Oh, maybe if we were out in the country you might get away with it, but not here in the city. Here in the city God knows that if you had really cried out for help someone would have come. That's why He hates girls like you so much, Miriam. He hates you so much that if anyone ever finds out what you did, you're going to be stoned to death. Stoned to death, Miriam! That's how much God hates you."

(*Still sobbing*) "I want to go home!"

"Yes, get dressed, go home, but you better hope your father never finds out what you did. At the very least he'll throw you out, and you won't last a week on the streets. Still, I can't stand the thought of the blood of even a girl like you on my hands. So, if he throws you out, you can come back here. I'll find a use for you."

I got dressed in my old homespun. Just as I got to the door, Simon threw some coins at me. "Here, give these to your father. Tell him they're in payment for what you gave away today."

I gathered the coins and I left. I thought, "I didn't give anything away. You stole it. You stole my innocence. You stole my trust. You stole my future," because I knew no man would ever want me now.

I used the money to buy food for my family. That night we had a feast unlike any we had ever had before. My brothers and sisters were so excited, but Dad just sat there staring at me as if he knew what had happened.

"Simon again?"

"Yes, Father, Simon."

"Why does Simon keep giving you all these things?"

"He didn't give them to me. I earned them."

"Aha, and I know HOW you earned them!"

"No, Father, it wasn't like that."

"Shut up!" he cried, and he slapped me across the face just like Simon had. "I know what kind of a man Simon is, but I never thought you'd give into him."

"Father, please, if you'd just listen. It wasn't like that. You don't understand."

"I understand that you are nothing more than a common whore and you are no longer my daughter."

"Father, please," I cried, but he wouldn't listen. He just kept hollering and hitting. My brothers tried to intervene, but it was of no use. As I bid a tearful farewell to my sisters, I warned them to never trust any man, least of all a Pharisee.

Then I left. I found a corner in which to hide, and I started to cry. I cried for my lost innocence. I cried for my lost family. I cried for my lost future, the husband and children I would never have. When I had cried every last tear, the void that was left began to fill with anger and hatred. I hated Simon for what he had done to me. I hated my father for not showing any kind of understanding or forgiveness. I hated myself for being so stupid as to think I could ever own anything nice.

And I hated God: that mighty God of Israel who dwells in the Holy of Holies never venturing out to see the plight of His people. A God who is more concerned with rosemary sprigs and sesame seeds than He is with the poor. A God whose ears are so filled with the prayers of the pious He cannot hear the cries of His children. A God who claims to be the God of Law but is in fact the God of loopholes.

By the morning, I knew that Simon was right. I never would last a week on the streets. So, I went back to his house. He greeted me with that same self-satisfied smirk. How could I have ever thought he had a nice smile? "*So,* daddy found out and threw you out, did he? Well, I can't say that I blame him. No man wants a slut for a daughter. Still, like I said, I can't bear the thought of even the blood of a girl like you on my hands, so, yeah, I'll take you in. But you have to do everything I tell you."

And I did. And I got to be very good at it. So good in fact, that Simon began to share me with his friends. Oh, but it was all right, God understood. They had needs. Simon is single, but he still had needs. This man's wife was ill, but he still had needs. This man's wife just gave birth, but he still had needs. I could never understand why God was so understanding about them and their needs but hated me so much for being the tool they used to satisfy those needs.

Then one day I was with another of Simon's friends. His wife was away tending to her dying mother, but he still had needs. While he was satisfying those needs, suddenly the door burst open and in came an angry mob of Pharisees, yelling terrible, obscene things at us. They dragged us out of bed barely giving me time to cover myself. The next thing I knew, I was in the middle of a Temple courtyard surrounded by a mob of people screaming for blood.

"The Law of God says adulterers must be stoned to death!"

My one small thought of comfort was, "Well, at least I won't be dying alone." I looked around to see the expression on the man's face with whom I was to die, but he wasn't there. Then I saw him, in the crowd yelling right along with the rest of them.

That's when the total absurdity of the situation struck me: I was to be stoned to death for committing adultery alone! I started to laugh hysterically. I turned my back on the crowd because I knew that laughter would soon turn to tears, and I wasn't about to give any of them the satisfaction of seeing me cry. I plastered myself up against a stone wall; a wall as cold and as hard as God's heart. I waited.

The arguing continued. The Law of God says that adulterers must be stoned to death, but the law of Rome forbids us from doing it. So, what do we do? Do we obey the law of God, or do we obey the law of Rome?

Then the true horror of the situation hit me. There wasn't a man there who cared anything about me or what I had done. Not one of them even saw me as a human being. To them I was just a test case to see how far they could push Rome.

Then I heard Simon's voice, "Well, what about, Jesus? Do we obey God, or do we obey Caesar?"

They're actually asking some man's opinion? A small spark of hope began to flicker. Maybe, just maybe, here was a man who would show a little bit of understanding, a little compassion.

We waited for what seemed like a lifetime. Then I heard His voice, "Let he who is without sin cast the first stone."

Oh, great, there's some defense. They all think they're without sin. I braced myself waiting for that first stone to hit; waiting even more anxiously for that last stone, the one that would finally end this miserable life. Then I could stand before God and tell Him exactly what I thought of Him: this mighty God of Israel who dwells in the Holy of Holies never venturing beyond its walls to see the plight of His people. This God who is more concerned with rosemary sprigs and sesame seeds than He is for the poor. This God whose ears are so filled with the prayers of the pious that He cannot hear the cries of His children; for I cried out for help, but no one came for me. I have heard other girls crying for help, but no one came for them either. This God of the Law who thinks it is somehow justice for a woman to be stoned to death for committing adultery alone.

Finally, I heard the sound of the first stone hitting the ground, but it hadn't touched me. The fools! They can't even hit me! Come on, come on, let's get this over with. Then more stones were hitting the ground, but none of them were coming anywhere near me. I heard the crowd beginning to disperse, but I was afraid to look around for fear of what I might see.

As the courtyard grew quiet, I felt a man's hands tugging at my dress, but He wasn't trying to pull it down, He was pulling it up, helping me cover myself. I looked at Him. His face was filled with compassion, and, dare I use the word, grace.

He smiled, "Well, it doesn't look like any of them could condemn you. I don't condemn you either."

"But I'm a whore!"

"No, you're not." He bent down, picked up a stone and put it in my hand. "You were a whore, but these stones have killed the woman you had been."

I said, "But you don't understand, you don't know all the things I have done."

"Come here," He said, and led me over to a place in the court yard. "What do you see written in the dirt there?"

"I don't see anything at all. "

"That's right, you don't. I had written something there. What it was doesn't matter. It was strictly between God and me. Now I have erased it. No one will ever know what it said. That's the way it is with your sins: they were strictly between God and you, and I have erased them. You have a new life. It is up to you to decide what to do with it." With that, He turned and started to leave. The men with Him began to follow, some of them smiling at me and wishing me well.

One of the women with Him came up to me. She took off her cloak and wrapped it around me. "He's really something, isn't He?"

Yes," I said, "Who is He?"

"That's Jesus. He's in the business of giving people new lives. I know just how you're feeling. You're amazed, overawed, wondering if it could be true, frightened about what to do with your future. Well, if I were you, and come to think of it, I've been you, I would follow Him."

"Oh, no, He doesn't want the likes of me."

"You are exactly the kind of person He wants. I should know. I was possessed by seven demons. They made me do terrible, awful things, but He drove them out. Now, all I want to do is to follow Him, to learn from Him, to serve Him."

"Oh, but the demons made you do what you did; I did mine of my own free will."

She said, "I doubt that very much. You may not have had the physical demons I did, but I would be willing to wager you had your own demons: Demons of poverty and want, demons of ignorance and need, demons of innocence, and trust, and dreams. Indeed, those are the most dangerous demons of all because Satan can so easily get his claws in them and use them to tear us apart."

At that point another woman came up. I recognized her as Joanna. Her husband was one of Herod's stewards. She said, " I noticed your gown was rather badly torn. I think you can wear one of mine. Here, try it on."

They held up the cloak while I slipped into my new gown.

"Mary's right, you know, you should come with us. After all, if you find you don't like us, you're free to leave."

If I don't like THEM, I free to leave? I hadn't been free to do anything for a very long time, and I really didn't see any other options. I certainly couldn't go back to Simon and that way of life, so I went with them.

That night I got to be the one to hand Jesus His meal. I was scared. First of all, I didn't know how He would react to seeing me there. Secondly, I really didn't think He would take food from my hand.

When He looked up at me, He broke into a big grin. "Miriam," He cried, "Oh, Miriam, I am so glad you've come to join us. Look everyone, it's Miriam. Come and greet your new sister. Make her feel at home."

"Sister"? "Home"? Two words I had not used in a very long time. However, they did make me feel welcome, like I was one of them.

A few days later, an invitation came from Simon for Jesus to join him for dinner. Now, I knew Simon better than anyone else there, and I knew he was up to something. So, I tried to warn Jesus.

He just smiled, "Thank you, Miriam, but I know exactly what kind of a man Simon is, and I can handle him. Trust me."

And I did.

As the time came for Jesus to go to Simon's I found I simply could not go in that house. It was filled with too much pain, too many ghosts. So, I stood outside with the crowd watching what was happening.

When Jesus entered, Simon didn't greet Him with a kiss. He didn't have Him anointed. He didn't even have His feet washed, a common ceremony of greeting for an honored guest. I should know, I had to perform it often enough. Then he had Jesus seated opposite him, not in a place of honor.

As the meal began, I could hear the Pharisees talking among themselves. Oh, they couldn't wait to see Simon take this imposter down a peg or two. What kind of man was this? He touches lepers; he eats with prostitutes and then claims to speak for God?

After a while I could bear it no longer. I burst into the room. I was going to tell them exactly what kind of a man He is. He is a man who sees with eyes of God. Yes, He touches lepers. Yes, he eats with prostitutes because He sees us as people of value. As I ran towards Him our eyes met, and I saw an almost imperceptible shake of His head. He didn't want me there. He didn't need me to defend Him. I was embarrassing Him! It was the last thing I wanted to do.

I fell to ground at His feet and began to cry. Years of tears flowed forth. When they began to wash away the dirt, I saw how calloused His feet were, and I started to kiss them. Then I remembered a small vial of ointment I had. I took it out, broke it, and began to pour it over His feet, the sweet fragrance permeating the room. Then I began to dry His feet with my hair. This same hair that all the men loved to run their fingers through, I was running through His toes.

That really started the gossiping going. "Look at this! What kind of a prophet is He who doesn't even know what kind of a woman she is?"

Then I knew that all I succeeded in doing was to add fuel to their fire. I was so ashamed of myself.

Suddenly I felt His hand on my head, comforting, reassuring. He wasn't upset. He wasn't embarrassed. I was His, and He would defend me.

"Simon," He said, "I have a story for you."

"Speak."

"Once there were two men who owed a certain creditor money. One owed him five denarii, a sum easily repaid by the selling of a few lambs. The other owed him five hundred denarii, a sum he would never be able to repay in his life. However, the creditor forgave both debts.

Now which of the two men do you think loved him more?"

Simon hesitated sensing it was a trick question. "I supposed the one who owed him the greater debt."

"You have spoken wisely," Jesus said. Then He cupped my face in His hands. "When I came in, you didn't greet me with a kiss, yet this woman has not stopped kissing my feet. You didn't have me anointed, yet this woman has anointed me with the sweetest of ointments. You didn't even have my feet washed, yet this woman has bathed them with her tears and dried them with her hair. This woman, whose sins were many, knows she is forgiven and so she loves greatly." Then He stood up and helped me to my feet. "Simon, it's been delightful, but I have had enough. Come, Miriam, let's go."

He helped me up and took me by the hand. He led me out past the dumbfounded Pharisees and past the laughing cheering crowd. When we got outside the perimeter, He turned. He was laughing, "Oh, Miriam, thank you. Thank you for preaching a better sermon than I could have ever preached alone!" Then He hugged me, and I knew I would never leave Him.

And I never did. I was there at the foot of the cross when He was crucified. I was among the women who went to the tomb that morning and found it empty. I was in the room when He suddenly appeared to us. I watched as He was lifted into heaven and heard Him promise to return once more. I was in that upper room the day the wind and the fire of the Holy Spirit engulfed and empowered us.

Oh, those first days of the early church were so exciting! People came by the thousands to join us, and I helped minister to them.

Then one day, I saw in the crowd my brothers and sisters. I went running to them for a joyous reunion until they stepped aside, and there stood my father. I stopped dead in my tracks. All the memories of that terrible night came flooding back. (*Anger building with each sentence.*) Why didn't he listen to me? Why didn't he show any kind of understanding or forgiveness?

How could he just throw me out like that?

The chains of anger and pain wrapped themselves around me like snakes. I couldn't move. I could barely breathe. Suddenly, I felt the stone in my pouch; the stone that Jesus had placed in my hands that day telling me the woman I had been was dead. I knew what I had to do. But it is so hard! Oh, Abba, Father, it is so hard, please help me!

Then in a moment of divine intervention, I saw my father wrapped in chains also: chains of guilt and regret. Somehow, I knew I held the key to both sets of chains. As my heart began to lighten, I smiled at him. "Father, it's good to see you. I'm so glad you've come." With that, both our chains fell to ground and disappeared in the dust.

He threw his arms open and I ran to him. "I'm sorry, Miriam," he cried, "I'm so sorry!"

"It's all right, Father. All is forgiven. Jesus has made everything new. Come, I want you to meet the rest of my family."

You see, that's what forgiveness does. It frees you from the past. It doesn't matter if you are the one that was hurt, or the one who did the hurting, forgiveness frees you both. Jesus gives you that power. He gives you that choice. You can choose to hold onto the past with all the pain and anger, all the sorrow and regret, or you can nail it to the cross and let it die there.

You can choose to remain in the dark hopelessness of the tomb, or you can walk through the door Jesus so graciously opens for us.

You can choose to stay enamored with the things of this world, aimlessly chasing after the latest fad, desperately seeking happiness, or you can follow Jesus into the kingdom of heaven and find true joy.

The choice is yours. Choose Jesus. Choose life! Amen.

POINTS TO PONDER FOR
THE SINFUL WOMAN

Read John 8:3-11; Luke 7:36-47

1. In this story, what dreams did Miriam have for her life?

2. How did her family situation influence those dreams?

3. How much control did she have over making those dreams come true?

4. What childhood dreams of yours have you achieved?

5. What dreams never came true?

6. Is there anything you could have done which might have changed the outcome?

7. How much of what happened to Miriam could she have prevented?

8. What might she have done differently?

9. At her lowest point, she became angry with everyone, including herself and God. Was her anger justified?

10. How might she have better dealt with what had happened?

11. Have you ever been angry with God because of some situation over which you felt you had no control?

12. How did you deal with that anger?

13. The scene in the courtyard brings an end to Miriam's first life. In the midst of her despair, anger and hopelessness, how did Jesus reach out to her?

14. In your darkest moments, how has Jesus reached out to you?

15. Mary Magdalene describes demons of "ignorance and need, poverty and want, and innocence, trust, and dreams." How is each of these demons at work in today's world?

16. What is the church's role in confronting these demons?

17. How can you help?

18. Simon treats Jesus with contempt when he invites Him to dinner. How do we see Jesus being treated with contempt in today's world?

19. How do Miriam's actions bring honor to Jesus?

20. What do you do to bring honor to Him?

21. Jesus praises Miriam for her repentance. How does knowing such repentance pleases Jesus help in your life?

22. When Miriam first sees her father, she is bound by chains of pain and anger. How does it help her to know her father is also bound by chains of regret and guilt help her to forgive him?

23. What divine help did she receive which enabled her to forgive?

24. How can forgiveness help both the one who has been hurt and the one who did the hurting?

25. Who do you need to forgive?

26. Do you believe Jesus can help you forgive?

MARTHA
OF BETHANY

Luke 10: 38-42; John 11: 17-44

(*Martha interacts with the audience, so some dialogue will change with the circumstances.*)

Good morning, my name is Martha. Can you all hear me all right? Lazarus tells me I have the kind of voice that be heard all over Bethany, but I want to make sure you can hear me, because every now and then I say something brilliant. It happens so rarely that I don't want anyone to miss it if does. If sometime during my story, you can't hear me, just give me a little wave. I'll probably wave back because I will have forgotten why I asked you to wave in the first place, but we'll get it all worked out.

(*If this is being told at a dinner use these lines. If not, skip straight to the part explaining she is noted for her hospitality*)

Have you all had enough to eat? If you haven't, I'm sure we can find something else. I worry about such things for two reasons. First, I am noted for my hospitality. Everybody knows that when you come to Martha's house, you're going to get fed and fed very well. Even the beggars know to come to my house. You see, the way I figure it, the good Lord has so blessed me and mine that it is only right we pass on those blessings to others. Besides, I know that people respond better to you when you feed them. So, everyone is full and happy, right?

Now, if you have been listening very carefully, you will have learned some very important things about me. First, my name is (*wait for a response*) Martha. And I live in the little village of (*wait for response*) Bethany, which is right outside of Jerusalem. And I live there with my brother (*wait for response*) Lazarus, who is one of the leading citizens in all of Bethany. And I also have a sister, (*usually they will call out Mary*) Mary. You've heard of Mary? Doesn't surprise me any; everybody's heard of Mary.

You see, Mary is everything I am not. Mary is pretty. Mary is witty. Mary knows just what to say to everyone to make them feel like they are THE most important person in the whole world at that particular moment. Me? I kind of get tongue-tied around people. Especially men. Now don't get me wrong; it's not that I don't like men, I just don't understand them. Their logic is so weird it simply escapes me. It's all right, though, because Lazarus tells me that men don't understand women either. Which rather begs the question: Why did God put us together in the first place? Do you ever wonder if He regrets that decision? I mean, think of how much more peaceful His whole existence would be if men and women weren't constantly trying to get along with one another.

But He made the decision, and we all live with the consequences.

Now I like children myself. I think children are absolutely the most wonderful way in the world to start out human beings, don't you? Children are welcomed in my kitchen anytime. They come in, and I'll teach them how to cook, and I'll tell them stories about our heritage. I'll tell them about, oh, Sarah and Abraham, Jacob and the ladder, Daniel in the lion's den. They like that one: How God made Daniel smell so bad not even the lions wanted to eat him!

I'll tell them about David and Goliath. They like that one, too: How little David with his small slingshot and mighty faith went up against the giant Goliath. Goliath started laughing at him, "Ho, ho, ho, is Israel sending out its dogs?"

Well, David took five little stones and put them in his slingshot, and twirling it around he cried, "For the glory of God and Israel," and let them fly. And POW! They hit Goliath right in the forehead. Goliath stopped laughing, and God started laughing because Goliath fell to the ground, and the ground shook, and he was dead! They really like that one.

Their favorite story, however, is Noah and the ark. Now the reason they like that one so much is because when I tell them that one, what I'll do is to bake a giant cookie in the shape of an ark and I'll give them each two little balls of cookie dough so they can make their own pairs of animals to go into the ark. We get the usual: we get the puppies and the kitties and the birdies and the bunny rabbits.

I had one little boy who wanted to make spider cookies. That might have been all right, except he wanted to put real spiders in them! I don't like spiders. I know they have a reason for being here, otherwise God would not have created them, but I don't know what it is. They just creep me out, all those legs going every which away. It's really neat, however, if you've ever watched a spider spinning a web. Have you ever seen a spider spinning a web? I have a friend who used to be a fisherman, but now he's a preacher. He told me that legend has it that fishermen actually learned how to make nets by watching spiders spin webs. I don't know if that's true or not, but at least it gives spiders a reason for being here. I did, however, put the kibosh on the little boy putting real spiders in my good cookie dough!

I had another little boy who wanted to make snake cookies. Now, I feel about snakes the same way I feel about spiders. I know they have a reason for being here, but I don't know what it is. I mean, you would have thought that with.as much trouble as that snake caused in the Garden of Eden, God never would have let them on the ark to begin with, but they're here, so He must have. Maybe that's their purpose. Maybe they show how truly forgiving God is. But whatever the reason for spiders and snakes, I am perfectly willing to share God's world with them, but not my kitchen! Either one of them comes into my kitchen, well, he'd best be on good terms with his creator because he's going to be meeting Him in a matter of minutes, I can tell you!

Well, anyway, because Lazarus is one of the leading citizens in all of Bethany, and because Mary likes

to flir... I mean Mary likes to talk to people, we do
a lot of entertaining. One of the people we like to
entertain most is a traveling rabbi from Nazareth by
the name of Jesus. Have you all heard of Him? (*Wait
for a response.*) Isn't He wonderful? (*Again, wait for a
response. If there isn't a big response say the following, if
there is skip this*) Ok, now by that response, or rather
lack thereof, I can determine one of three things:
Either you have never heard of Him and you're fibbing
to me, or you've heard of Him, but you don't think
He's wonderful, and I can hardly believe that, or you're
shy. Now I'm going to give you the benefit of the doubt
and say it was because you are shy, so I'm going to
give you another chance. DON'T BLOW IT! Isn't He
wonderful? (*This usually gets a good response.*)

Yeah, I think He's wonderful. He just makes
everything so understandable. He tells us about
God with stories. Like, He told this one story of the
shepherd who had lost a sheep. Leaving the ninety-
nine other sheep behind with the other shepherds, the
man went in search of this one poor little lost lamb.
He searched everywhere for this lamb. He searched
in high places and low places. He searched in smooth
places and rough places. He searched in straight
places and curvy places, all the while calling the lamb
by name. Finally, the shepherd heard the little lamb
baaing. Looking down over a steep cliff, the shepherd
saw the little lamb caught in a bramble bush. Risking
his own life, the shepherd climbed down and freed the
little lamb.

Cradling him gently in his arms he took him back
to the other sheep and the other shepherds where

there was much rejoicing because what had been lost had been found!

Now, I will be perfectly honest with you; I don't know a whole lot about shepherds. What I know about shepherds is that when they come down out of the mountains, they're hungry and they smell bad. Now I will feed them, but I am not going to breathe anywhere near them, I can tell you. So, I really didn't understand that story.

Then Jesus told us the story of the woman who had lost a coin. She searched everywhere for that coin. She searched through every drawer and every cupboard. She searched in every nook and every cranny. She even went so far as to light lamps in the middle of the afternoon so she could search through all the reeds on the floor, until finally, she found the lost coin. She took it out and she showed her neighbors, "Look, I have found the lost coin." There was much rejoicing because what had been lost had been found. And now she didn't have to tell her husband she lost it in the first place!

I understand that story, because I know how Lazarus gets when I do something like that. "Well, what did you do a dumb thing like that for, Martha?"

"Oh, I don't know, Lazarus. Maybe it's because I like to see your face turn red and your veins bulge out!" I mean, what does the man think, that I do these things on purpose?!

So, I understood that one.

Then Jesus went on and He told us the story of the father with the two sons. The younger son was really nasty. He asked for his share of the inheritance, which was the same thing as wishing his father were dead. Then he went out and he wasted it on wild women and wicked wine and raunchy songs and anything else he could find to waste it on he could find to waste it on until he was flat broke. I mean, this guy was reduced to feeding pigs-pigs for heaven sake-and wishing he could eat what he was feeding the pigs.

One day the young man finally came to his senses. He said, "You know what? Even the servants in my father's house have it better than I do. They have decent clothing, they're sleeping on clean linens, and they're not living on pig leftovers. Maybe, just maybe, if I go back and I apologize to my father, maybe out of the goodness and mercy of his heart, he'll hire me on as a servant. I know I've blown the whole son thing, but even as his servant I'd be better off than I am now." So, mustering all the courage and humility he could, the young man started back to his father's house.

The father, meanwhile, had never given up on his son. He thought about him every day. He prayed for him every day. And he watched for him every day. Until finally, on that one fateful morning, the father looked down the road and he saw this poor bedraggled figure limping up the road, and he recognized him as his son. Forgetting all rules of dignity and decorum, the father went running down the road to welcome his son home. As he approached, the son began the speech he had so very carefully prepared, "Father, I have sinned against heaven and against you..."

But the father interrupted him, "it's all right, my boy. All is forgiven. You're home now. Let's party!"

So, they went into the house and they started to party!

Now, the older boy, meanwhile, had been out in the fields working. He came in to find this party going on, so he called for a servant, (*Whistle*) "*Come* here. What's happening?"

The servant said, (*Happy and excited*) "Your brother's come home, so we're partying!"

Well, that sent the older boy into a major funk, I can tell you. He started to pout. He refused to go into the party. The father, forgetting all rules of dignity and decorum went out to talk to the older son. "Son, what's the matter?"

"What's the matter? What is the matter? I'll tell you what's the matter. That son of yours asks for his share of the inheritance, which may I remind you is the same thing as wishing you were dead. Then he goes out and wastes it on wild women and wicked wine and raunchy songs, and anything else he could find to waste it on. Then when he's flat broke, he comes crawling back to you, and you welcome him home like a conquering hero.

"Meanwhile, me, the good son, I have stayed here all this time. I have worked for you. I have followed every one of your rules and regulations, yet you have never even offered me so much as a kid to celebrate with my friends."

The father looked at the boy and said, "Son, don't you understand? You have been with me always. You could have had a party anytime you wanted it; all you would have had to do was ask. But your brother, YOUR BROTHER, was lost, but now he is found. He was dead, but now he is alive. That is something truly worth celebrating."

Jesus never told us if the older boy ever went into the party. I think he wanted us think about what we would do. Between you and me and the gatepost, I have always had a secret sympathy for that older boy, because I know what it is like to be the one that does all the work and have the other one have all the fun However, then I realized that that parable isn't about the two sons at all, because neither one of them was behaving the way they should. Oh, it's easy to see the sins of the younger boy, but the older one was just as much of a prodigal. You see, even though he stayed with his father, he never truly understood his father: not his grace, not his goodness, not his generosity nor his love.

No, the parable is all about the father, and how he loved his two sons, not because of the things they did or didn't do, but simply because they were his sons. You see, there was nothing that younger son could ever do that was so bad that it would make his father stop loving him; nothing so terrible that he couldn't come home and find forgiveness, and grace and love. And there was nothing that older boy could ever do that was so good it would make his father love him anymore, because he couldn't. He already loved him as much as possible simply because he was his son.

That's the way God is with us. He doesn't love us because of the things we do or don't do. He loves us because we are His. There is nothing we can ever do that is so bad it would make God stop loving us; nothing so terrible that we can't come home and find forgiveness, and grace, and love. And there is nothing we can ever do that is good that it could possibly make God us love us even one iota more, because He can't. He already loves as much as possible simply because we are His children.

Anyway, one of the last times Jesus came to visit, I could tell just by looking at Him that there was something very heavy weighing on His mind. He looked so tired, so preoccupied as if He were facing a major decision and was turning it over and over in His mind. So, I decided to make Him a wonderfully large meal. Now, as all you ladies must know, and maybe some of you men, when you make a wonderfully large meal, there is a whole of work and a whole lot of dishes.

And where was my loving sister while I was doing all this work? She was out there, sitting next to Jesus asking Him all these dumb questions. Couldn't the woman see how tired He was?

Couldn't she see how much work there was to do?

After a while, I decided she had had just about enough of Jesus' attention, and I certainly needed the help, so I went out and leaned down and very quietly said, "Mary, would you please come help me in the kitchen?"

To which she very loudly responded, "No, leave me alone. Can't you see I'm talking to Jesus?"

(*Shrug shoulders*) I thought I'd try it again. "But I really could use some help with the dishes."

That's when Jesus looked at me and said, "Martha, leave Mary alone. She understands what's important."

Well, I was crushed! He had never spoken to me like before. I had never heard Him speak to anyone like that before. I was angry, and I was hurt! So, I did what I always do when I'm angry and hurt: I fled to my kitchen.

Now, I don't know about the rest of you ladies here, but when I get angry and hurt, I tend to mumble a lot. Are any of you here mumblers? (*Someone will agree. Speak to her*) Do you bang things around, also? (*She usually agrees, so happily cry*) "Oh, sister!"

I'll tell you; I am one of the all-time great mumblers and bangers of things. So, I would like you to picture, if you will, my kitchen; me at the sink full of dirty dishes, unhappily mumbling and banging away sounding something like this: (*washing imaginary dishes*) "Right! Leave Mary alone! Mustn't let Mary get her hands in all this dirty dish water. Why, they might turn red and rough. Can't have that for good old Mary. Doesn't matter about Martha. Mary is just so smart. Mary understands what's important. Martha doesn't understand anything. (*pause and tap toes*) Right! I'll bet you if supper time would have come around and there had been no food on the table, they would have had another idea about what was important and what wasn't. Of course, it wouldn't have mattered. All I would have had to do was put a bowl of water in front of Him, and He could have turned it into chicken soup!"

That's when I heard his voice behind me, "Oh, Martha, I don't think I could ever make soup as good as yours."

Oh, man, He's not supposed to be hearing this! What's He doing in my kitchen anyway? Lazarus doesn't even know where the kitchen is, for crying out loud. Now, not only am I angry and hurt, I'm embarrassed. I couldn't even look at Him. I just went back to doing my dishes. The next thing I know, He's standing beside me with a dish towel in His hands, drying the dishes! Now never in all my born days have I seen a man dry a dish. I looked at Him and my mouth fell open.

He just shrugged, " Mom always made me help with the dishes." Well, who was I to argue with Mom?

So, there we are in my kitchen, me washing and Him drying. Now, I will tell you, the mumbling had stopped. The banging, however, continued. (*Continue washing the dishes with gusto*)

After a few moments of this, He said to me, "Martha, I believe you may be upset about something."

"OH, never could fool You, could I?"

"All right, Martha, what's wrong?"

Well, I wasn't going to say anything, but He just has this way about Him that makes you want to open up to Him, so I very calmly and rationally explained to Him what was bothering me. (*Speaking rapidly in a very angry and excited voice*) "You want to know what's wrong? I'll tell you what's wrong. Mary, that's what's wrong. I mean, I know how hard you work when you're on the road, and I know you don't eat properly, so when you come here, I try to create a place of peace and rest for you. I try to get good food in you, and it's not easy cooking for you and all your men. I mean, Peter alone eats like an army! And look at all these dishes I have to do! And where is my loving sister while I am doing all this work? She is out there, sitting on her fat (*pause as if looking for the proper word*) cushion asking You all these dumb questions, while I am in here with all these dumb dishes. I work and I slave and the first time I ask for a little bit of help, I thought you, of all people, You who's always talking about how we should help one another and bear each other's burdens, I thought you would be on my side. But no! You're just like everybody else. You take her side, too. Everybody's always worried about Mary, Mary, Mary, and nobody ever worries about Martha and that's what's bothering me. Thank you very much."

My bags were already packed for the guilt trip I knew I was about to be sent on, but I didn't care, because it felt good!

Instead, He very quietly said to me, "Martha, who am I?"

"Who am I?" That was a question for which I was not prepared. "Who do you think you are?" That was the question for which I was prepared, but "Who am I?"

I looked at Him and said, "Why, you're Jesus!"

"Is that all?"

Now, I had been listening a lot more than anyone ever gave me credit for, and I had formed my own ideas about who this man is. I said, "No. No, you are the Messiah, the promised one of God. That is why it is so important to me to serve you, because in serving you I am serving God."

He took my hands out of the dish pan and held them up. I remember thinking how ridiculous we must look with dirty dishwater running down our arms and dripping off our elbows. He looked at me and said, "Mary doesn't understand that yet. That is why it is so important for her to be out there asking me all those questions."

He went on, "Martha, I love coming here. You do, indeed, create a place of peace and rest for me. And your food? Martha, your food is the best I've ever eaten, including Mom's; don't you tell her I said that! But Martha, I cannot allow you or anyone else to stand in the way of someone seeking the truth. Your comfort and mine are nothing compared to someone's salvation. Now, do you understand what I'm saying?"

I nodded, because I thought I did. Then He gave me a hug, and He gave me a kiss, and He started towards the kitchen door. I was feeling a bit braver by then so I looked at Him and said, "What? You're not going to help with the rest of the dishes?"

He just started laughing that wonderful musical laugh of His, and He came back and helped with the rest of the dishes! We just had a high old time in my kitchen that night. We talked, and we laughed, and we even sang a little bit. I got to ask Him all those questions I never would have had the nerve to ask in front of anyone. I learned a lot that night. I learned a lot about God, and I learned a lot about Him, and I learned a lot about me. I even learned a lot about Lazarus and Mary.

Those lessons come home to me a little while later when Lazarus became very, very ill. We knew that

Jesus was in the vicinity, so we sent word to Him that Lazarus was ill, expecting Him to come and heal him. But He didn't come.

Mary began to panic, "Where is He? Why isn't He coming?"

I said, "I don't know, Mary. He has a reason. He'll be here. Just trust Him."

But Lazarus became even sicker, and still Jesus didn't come. Mary began to panic even more, " Where is He? Why isn't He here?"

I said, "I don't know. He has a reason. He always has a reason. Just trust Him."

Finally, Lazarus died. Mary just fell apart. She rent her cloak, she began wailing, the entire village came in to mourn with her. And me? I fled to my kitchen because that's where I go when I'm upset, and somebody was going to have to feed all those people.

As I worked, I kept thinking, "Why didn't He come? He has a reason. He always has a reason, but what could it possibly be?"

After about four days, I looked out the door and there I saw Jesus walking down the road surrounded by His disciples. I got all excited and ran in, and cried, "Mary, Mary, He's coming, He's coming!"

She looked up and said, " Who's coming?"

I said, "Jesus is coming!"

She said, "So?"

I said, "Aren't you even going to go greet Him?"

"No, why should I? He's too late."

I said, "Well, I'm going to go greet Him."

I ran up to Him and I said, " Lord, Lord, our brother has died, but even now if you choose, you could help him. So, please, choose to help Lazarus."

He looked at me and said, "You truly believe that, don't you Martha?"

I said, "I believe you can do anything you want to do, so please want to help Lazarus."

He looked around, "Where's Mary?"

"She's in the house. She thinks you're too late."

And He smiled at me, "Now do you understand what we talked about in your kitchen?"

And I did! You see, even with all the questions Mary had been asking Him, she still didn't understand who this man is nor the power He possesses. But she was going to learn. As a matter of fact, we were all going to learn that day.

We started down towards the house and finally Mary came out. She walked up to Jesus and said, (*angrily*) "Our brother is dead. If you had been here, he wouldn't have died."

I looked at Jesus and there were tears in His eyes. You know, I have never been sure if those tears were there because of Lazarus, which is what everyone else thought, or if they were there because of Mary's lack of faith, which is what I think.

Jesus asked us where Lazarus was buried, so we took Him to the tomb. He ordered the stone to be rolled away.

I said, "Wait a minute, he's been dead for four days now. There is bound to be a terrible stench coming out of that tomb!"

Jesus just laughed at me, "Always the pragmatist, aren't you Martha? Are you sure you want me to do this?"

I thought about it, and then I figured that any man who could conquer death could certainly conquer the stench of it, right? So, I said, "Yes, go ahead. Do it."

The stone was rolled away. Jesus looked up to heavens and thanked God for what was about to happen. Then He called our brother's name. Out of that tomb walked our brother, alive and well.

Mary went rushing to Lazarus to rip off his grave clothes, and I just stood there thanking Jesus for what He had done for us. You see, He had taken the tears of sorrow and turned them into tears of joy. He had taken the food of mourning and turned it into a feast of celebration. He had proven to everyone that God is more powerful than anything, even death itself.

There was no shutting Mary up after that. She would tell anyone who would listen and even those who didn't want to listen about what Jesus had done for us. And me? I just went right on cooking and serving. We made a pretty good pair. I fed their bodies and she fed their souls.

Both are important, because after all, how can a man hear the good news if his stomach's growling too loudly, right?

Well, I learned a lot from Jesus. I learned that not everyone comes to know the Lord in the same way. Some of us love Him with our hearts, and then begin to understand Him with our heads. Others understand Him with their heads and then begin to love Him with their hearts. Because the human head, generally speaking, is harder than the human heart, it may take those folks a bit longer, but it doesn't really matter, as long as you come to know the Lord with all of your mind and love Him with all of your heart.

And I learned that we all serve the Lord in different ways, because we are all given different graces and talents. Some of us feel very comfortable standing up in front of people talking about what Jesus has done for us. Others of us prefer serving in the, shall we say more practical aspects of ministry. But it really doesn't matter, because whatever gift, grace or talent God has given you, it is because He knows it's needed in this world. What does matter is that you take that gift and use it for His glory, so that His kingdom may be established here as it is in heaven.

Finally, I learned that no one has the right to stand the way of anyone else's faith journey. After all, we have no idea from where they are coming, nor any idea where the Lord is leading. Instead, we must concentrate on our own faith journey.

That is my prayer for you this day: That you come to know the Lord with all your mind, that you love Him with all your heart, and that you serve Him with all your being. Walk closely with Him. May the light of His countenance shine upon you, and in you and through you to a world that is sorely in need of His grace, His love and His mercy. Amen.

(*As you begin to leave*) Oh, I almost forgot, if you truly wish to follow in the footsteps of our Lord, make sure you help with the dishes!

God bless you always.

POINTS TO PONDER FOR
MARTHA

Read Luke 10: 38-42; John 11: 17-44

1. Martha loved to cook and serve. How did she use this passion to serve the Lord?

2. What is your passion?

3. How can you use it to serve the Lord?

4. Mary is more the intellectual type, loving to sit, listen and learn. How did she serve the Lord?

5. With whom do you more closely relate?

6. How do you use your abilities and preferences to improve your relationship with Jesus?

7. Which characteristic of the other woman do you most admire? How could you become more like her?

8. At the dinner for Jesus, Martha became upset that Mary wasn't helping her. Why was she so angry?

9. Have you ever become angry because you felt the work you do goes unnoticed?

10. How do you deal with that anger?

11. When Lazarus became ill, Jesus didn't immediately respond to the sisters' request; why?

12. Have you ever experienced a time when God didn't immediately respond to a prayer?

13. How did you feel about it?

14. What did you do?

15. When Jesus finally arrived, Lazarus had been dead for four days. How did each of the sisters react?

16. What were the reasons for their different responses?

17. John 11: 33-35 tells us Jesus was deeply moved and wept. What do you think brought Jesus to tears?

18. Do you think there are situations today which bring Him to tears?

19. John 11: 37 says some people questioned why Jesus didn't save Lazarus. Do you ever question God's actions in your life or the lives of others?

20. How do you handle such feelings?

21. Jesus doesn't act until Martha agreed to have the stone rolled away. Do think there are times when God doesn't act because we don't allow it?

22. Lazarus had to walk out of the tomb on his own and needed help to be freed of his grave clothes. Do we have any responsibilities when asking God for something to happen in our lives?

23. Are there any things which we need to remove or help someone else remove to find new life in Jesus?

24. Read John 12: 1-7. Judas Iscariot becomes upset at Mary's extravagance in showing her love for Jesus. Have you ever been accused of being too extravagant in expressing your love for Jesus?

25. How did that make you feel?

26. In the benediction, Martha warned us to never stand in the way of anyone else's faith journey. Jesus referred to this as being a stumbling block. Have you ever fallen over such a stumbling block?

27. Have you ever been a stumbling block to someone?

THE
HUNCHED-OVER
WOMAN

Luke 13: 10-17

Good morning. My name is Lily. Lily of the Valley they call me, and it seemed like a very appropriate name because I was in that valley for a long, long time. Eighteen years they tell me. I don't know. To me it seemed like a lifetime. I couldn't remember the days when I could stand up straight and run and play like the other children. I do remember the teasing, the taunting, the name calling. I couldn't really blame them. After all, they learned it from their parents. I never understood why no one could see that beneath that misshapen hulk I was the same as everyone else. I had feelings to be hurt, needs to be met, the desire to be loved.

Fortunately, my family created a safe haven for me: a place where I was protected, encouraged, cherished. Many were the times my brother Jacob got into a fight when the teasing went one step too far. Often my sister Rose would join the fracas. When we got home, there would be the mandatory reprimand, but beneath the words was the tone of approval, almost pride that they would stand up for their little sister. For their parts, my parents never allowed me to use my physical disabilities as excuses for not at least trying something. Dad carved me a strong sturdy walking stick out of an old grapevine and then cheered me on as I learned to maneuver with it. Mom used to tell me, "Lily, you can't do everything, but you can do some things. Never let your disabilities stand in the way of your abilities and never allow your failures to overshadow your successes." So, she taught me to do those things which I could do; spinning and sewing because you didn't have to sit up straight to accomplish those.

But my favorite chore of all was the gardening. Oh, how I loved being in my garden. It was my own personal sanctuary. When I felt the dirt between my fingers and toes, it was as if God and I were working hand in hand to care for His creation. I quickly learned to discern between the productive plants and those that had to be removed so as to not stunt the growth of the healthy plants. I learned to care for delicate little roots and tender little shoots so they would grow strong and sturdy. I learned what to mix into the soil to nourish the plants and make them even more productive. I learned what flowers to plant around my garden to discourage pests who wanted to come in and share in my bounty.

All my hard work paid off. Mom use to tell me, "Lily, we have the finest vegetables in the whole village." My heart would warm, because I had a gift: a gift that was accepted and appreciated.

I also learned about herbs and spices: which ones best flavored which vegetables, what could be used to settle an upset tummy, what leaves could be crushed and rubbed on a rash to make it stop itching, and what ones when applied to a cut or scrape would make it heal faster. Soon word of my knowledge began to spread. People began coming to me for advice and help. I always gave it to them.

Dad would get so frustrated with me. "Lily," he'd say, "They treat you so badly, they're always so mean to you. How can you possibly be so kind to them?"

"Oh, Dad," I'd say, "They don't understand. Maybe by being kind to them they'll learn not to judge people by outside appearances but rather to look into the heart just like God does."

He would grunt, and I could almost hear his head shake, but Rose would whisper to me, "He's smiling at you, Lily. Daddy's smiling at you." And I knew I had taught him a lesson, also.

I had another talent developed as a child: I could tell people's profession by their feet. It was a game Rose and I use to play. She was amazed at how good I was at it, but it really wasn't that hard. You see, certain professions have certain tell - tale marks.

Women's feet were generally smaller and those that were broad and flat were the feet of busy mothers chasing after wayward children.

Shepherd's feet were tinged with green with blades of grass stuck between their toes from all the meadows through which they walked to feed their flocks. They also had a rather distinctive aroma from the more unsavory things through which they trod.

Fishermen feet showed signs of splinters having been pulled out and they always walked with a rolling motion and stood with their feet planted far apart as if constantly balancing on a rocking boat. They had the distinctive odor of fish about them that never truly washed away.

Carpenters feet showed signs of scars on the top of the foot and usually a broken toe or two from where tools or stone or wood had been dropped during the practice of their professions. They had that sweet smell of fresh sawdust clinging to them.

And then there were the feet of the high and mighty leaders of the synagogue. Those oh so pampered feet that were nightly rubbed with costly and aromatic oils. No sign of corns or calluses on those feet. Nothing to show they ever did a day's work in their lives.

I had dreams like other people, too, although mine were different. My dreams were much simpler, yet harder to achieve. You see, I dreamed of one day feeling the wind in my face instead of down my back. I dreamed of having rain rolling down my cheeks, rain that fell from the sky and not from my eyes.

I dreamed of one day looking into the faces of my family to see if their hearts reflected the words I heard. Oh, Rose assured me that they did, but still I wanted to see it for myself. I wanted to see the pride in my father's eyes for all the things I had accomplished tinged with a little bit of sorrow for the things I would never have.

I wanted to see the fire in my mother's eye: Those dangers that would flash out whenever anyone would dare to accuse me of being a sinner. I was her daughter and they better never treat me as anything less.

I wanted to see the stubborn resolution in my brother's eyes, the challenge that said I was part of the family and anyone who wanted to be around him had better accept me as part of the package.

But my dream above all dreams was to one day see a rainbow. Rose told me about them; how even while the rain was still falling the sun would break through the clouds and there would appear in the sky a beautiful arc of color, a shimmering promise that the storm was ending, and God was still in control. Oh, how I wanted to see that rainbow! We even went so far as to plant one in the corner of my garden. Rose helped me pick out the flowers which best reflected the colors she saw, but it wasn't the same. I wanted to see that arc in the sky, to know my own storm was ending and God was still in control.

I had my fears, also. My biggest fear was that I would somehow outlive my parents. What would happen to me then? Would I be thrown out of my home, banished from my garden, forced to live on the street at the mercy of those who always took such great delight in tormenting me? Oh, Rose promised me I would always have a home with her, but women don't always have much of a say over who lives in their own houses. Jacob, too, swore I would always have a home with him, but I had known other women who had so mercilessly nagged their husbands that they went back on a promise just to obtain a little peace in their own homes. Is that what would happen to me?

Then one day Leah, Jacob's intended, came and sat down next to me. "Lily," she said, "I have a question for you."

Oh no, I thought, here it comes: the list of excuses as to why I shouldn't hold Jacob to his promise, the litany of rational explanations as to why it wouldn't be a good idea or even fair.

"Lily," she said, "Jacob tells me that if I marry him, you come as part of the package, that you will always have a home with us. Now, Lily, what I want to know is this: Can you ever accept me as part of the package? Could you ever truly think of me as your sister?"

The storm behind my eyes broke and rain began streaming down my checks. I tried to nod, but in my condition, it never really came out right. But Leah understood. She put her arm around me, giggled a little and said, "I'll take that as a yes."

"Oh yes," I cried, "Yes! Yes! Yes!" She put her cheek against mine and I felt the rain on her face, also. From that moment on, she was the sister of my heart.

Well, I did indeed outlive my parents, but true to their words, Jacob and Leah took me in. It was wonderful. My little nieces and nephews knew that Aunt Lily may look different, but Aunt Lily was pretty special. Aunt Lily knew just what to do to settle an upset tummy. Aunt Lily knew what to rub on a rash to make it stop itching. Aunt Lily knew what to put on a scrape or a cut to make it heal faster. And Aunt Lily was a good listener. You could tell her anything: all your joys and sorrows, your triumphs and tragedies, all of the terrible indignities and injustices suffered at the hands of your parents or other adults. Aunt

Lily would listen, and she would sympathize, and she would try to explain things, and help out if she could. And Aunt Lily always had something good to eat.

Every Sabbath I would go to the synagogue to worship and present my offering, and every Sabbath it was the same story. Those oh so pampered aromatic feet of the high and mighty leaders of the synagogue would block my way.

"Get away from here, woman. You don't belong here."

"Please, I just want to worship my Lord."

"He doesn't want your worship. I mean, look at you! Nobody wants you here."

"But I have my offering. "

"Then leave it with us and get out. You are an abomination in the eyes of the Lord.»

So, I would leave my offering of herbs and spices and go home. Jacob would get so frustrated with me. "Lily," he would say, "why do you insist on going week after week? You know they don't want you there."

"Because, Jacob, I don't go for them. I go to worship my Lord. It is what He desires. It is what He deserves. That they choose to block my worship is not my problem. It is theirs and they will have to answer for it one day."

"But why do you insist on giving an offering? You know they just keep it and use it for their own pleasures."

"That's not my problem either. I don't give my offering to them, I give it to the Lord. That they choose to keep for themselves, to in fact steal from

God, is something else they will have to answer for someday."

And he would grunt, and I could almost hear his head shaking. But my niece would whisper, "He's smiling at you, Aunt Lily, Daddy's smiling at you." And I knew I had taught Jacob a lesson also.

(*Bend over and speak mostly to the floor.*)

Then one Sabbath everything changed. I had gone to the synagogue as usual, but the crowd was bigger than normal, the air charged with excitement. A small flicker of hope began to burn. Maybe, just maybe, I would be able to sneak in without anyone noticing and worship God as I want to worship Him. However, as I approached the door, those oh so pampered aromatic feet of the high and mighty leaders of the synagogue blocked my way. "Get away from here, woman. You don't belong here."

"Please, I just want to worship my Lord."

"He doesn't want your worship. I mean, look at you. Nobody wants you here."

"But I have my offering."

"Then leave it with us and get out. You are an abomination in the eyes of the Lord."

Oh, why can't they ever just leave me alone? Why do they have to torment me all the time? Do they think I want to look like this? Or maybe they're right. Maybe I am an abomination in the eyes of the Lord. Maybe I should just go back to my garden and eat worms and die. I turned and started to hobble away when I bumped headlong into someone. I began to fall, but these strong tender hands steadied me, and a kind and gentle voice said, "Oh, be careful now."

I looked down at His feet, but these were unlike any feet I had ever seen before. They seemed to be the feet of everyman. His toes were tinged with green, the feet of a shepherd, but He stood with them planted far apart as if balancing on a rocking boat, the feet of a fisherman. But wait, were those tiny scars on the top of His feet where tools or stone or wood had been dropped in practicing of carpentry? Yet, someone cared for these feet for they looked soft and smelled sweet as if oils were rubbed nightly into them.

The voices of the high and mighty leaders interrupted my musings. "What are you doing, Jesus? Just let her go. She doesn't belong here. If she wants healing, why can't she come back another day? Why does she have to disturb the Sabbath?"

Suddenly, that kind and gentle voice was filled with anger. "How dare you! This is a daughter of Abraham, yet you would deny her worship? If she was one of your lambs, you would care for her Sabbath or no Sabbath. You would give her food and water Sabbath or no Sabbath. Yet you would deny her the bread of life, the living water? If she were one of your oxen and had fallen into a ditch you would pull her out Sabbath or no Sabbath. You would tend to her wounds Sabbath or no Sabbath. Yet you would deny her healing? No. No. Enough is enough. Eighteen years she has suffered under this demon, and she will not suffer one day longer!"

With that, He rubbed His hands down my back. I felt myself straightening up. (*Begin to straighten up, until standing straight.*) Bones and muscles long since used to one position began to scream in protest. The pain! Oh, the pain! But it was such a good pain, a healing pain. My eyes moved up His legs, across His waist, over His chest until I was looking straight into His face. His eyes: the eyes of my family. My father's eyes, full of pride for all the things I had accomplished, tinged with a little bit of sorrow for the things I would never have. My mother's eyes, those fiery daggers flashing out at the high and mighty leaders of the synagogue. How dare they accuse me of being a sinner! I was a daughter of Abraham and they better never treat me as anything less. My brother's eyes, that stubborn resolution that said I was one of the family, and anyone who wanted to be around Him had better accept me as part of the package.

The storm behind my eyes had broken. Tears were streaming down my cheeks. Suddenly, the sun came out from behind a cloud. Its brightness nearly blinded me because I had never before looked so fully into the light. And that's when I saw it: the rainbow! Around His head, that beautiful ark of color, that shimmering promise that my storm was ending, and God was still in control!

My legs, unused to supporting my weight in this position began to crumble, but quickly His arms were around me. "Oh," He said, "Don't worry. I've got you. I'm not going to let you fall. Peter, John, come here and help your sister."

Then more arms were around me helping me stand, more words of encouragement were being whispered to me.

Then Jesus looked at those dumbfounded high and mighty leaders and very calmly asked, "Now, what were you saying?"

But of course, there were no words. Jesus' actions had said it all. He took me by the hand and led me past the laughing cheering crowd, past the furious fuming Pharisees and into the synagogue where for the first time in my life I could worship God as He is meant to be worshiped, with joy and thanksgiving.

After that, I decided that I wanted to follow Jesus and become one of His disciples. Oh, Jacob and Leah tried to talk me out of it, but deep down inside they understood. They knew that for the first time in my life I could decide where to go, what to do, how to live. For the first time I had a choice and I chose to follow Jesus.

It was wonderful. The disciples warmly welcomed me in and quickly found out what gifts and talents I had to offer. Soon they began coming to me for something to settle an upset stomach, an ointment to rub on a rash, or something to help a cut or scrap heal faster. Matters too small to bother the Master with. And they learned I had another talent also. I knew just how to rub tired aching feet to make them feel better. Oh, I was never allowed to do Jesus' feet. That honor was reserved for His mother. But I could do the other disciples. I remember one evening after a particularly busy day I was rubbing Peter's feet. He leaned back with a most contented sigh. "Ah, Lily," he said, "You have no idea what a wonderful gift this is." My heart warmed because I had a gift: A gift that was accepted and appreciated.

I had another talent, too; one that I didn't think was anything special because, indeed, every young girl was taught how to do this. One day Peter, John and I went into a village to buy some supplies. I took some of the money Judas Iscariot had given us and went to purchase some herbs on which I was running low. Peter and John went to buy some grain. When I met up with them, they were walking away from the stand shaking their heads. Peter was saying, " Nope. Sorry, too rich for our blood."

I just looked at them and said, "Wait a minute, fellows." I went back and in less than a minute I had more grain than we had come for, for less money than we had expected to spend.

Peter just stood there shaking his head and laughing. "John," he said, "we are in the presence of the master haggler!"

Again, my heart warmed, for this oh so simple everyday talent that all young girls were taught how to do was accepted and appreciated.

When we got to Jerusalem, I was overwhelmed by the city. It was grander and more diverse than anything I ever imagined. And the marketplace? I could spend hours just wandering around the marketplace looking at the all things I never knew existed, let alone knew I needed.

One day, as I was wandering, I heard a small whimper coming from down an alley way. I went back and there lay a young girl. She had been savagely attacked, brutally beaten, her body bruised and bleeding, her face filled with terror. I talked to her, calmly, reassuringly, until finally she allowed me to approach her. I examined her and realized she would never live to see the sunset, which was probably just as well since her mind had been even more badly abused than her body. I gave her something to ease the pain and I held her. I told her that it didn't matter what those men had done to her, God still loved her. He was preparing a place for her: a place where she would be protected, encouraged, cherished. I sang her the songs my mother use to sing to me when my own night terrors threatened to overwhelm; the songs I sang to my nieces and nephews when their own personal dragons rose up in attack.

Gradually, the terror left her face, but her eyes never left mine. Suddenly, they widened and filled with joy and wonder. Then she closed them for the last time.

I heard a noise behind me. I turned and there were those wonderful everyman's feet. I looked up at Him. He said, "She saw the rainbow, Lily. Around your head she saw the rainbow. She knew her storm was ending, and God was still in control. Thank you, Lily. Thank you for giving this, My child, the rainbow." With that He picked up her body and took her for proper burial.

I just sat there in utter amazement. You see, I had never told anyone about seeing the rainbow. It seemed like too precious a gift, too sacred a moment to share with anyone. But Jesus knew. He knew I had seen it; He knew what it meant to me, but most importantly, He knew I had given it to someone else.

That moment remains frozen in the memories of my mind. A time to which I can return whenever I am feeling particularly useless and unworthy. You see,

I have never preached a sermon that warmed 3,000 hearts. I have never been used as an instrument for a miracle. I have never planted a church that changed hundreds of lives. But I can help those who do.

You must understand, the kingdom of heaven is not some large geo-political entity ruled over by those interested only in power and wealth. Rather, the kingdom of heaven is made up of people, brought together by a common belief and bound together by a common love. People; each with their own unique talents, abilities, graces, gifts. Gifts that will be accepted and appreciated. For in the words of my mother, echoed in the teachings of Jesus, " You can't do everything, but you can do some things. Never let your disabilities stand in the way of your abilities. And never let your failures overshadow your successes."

Remember, everyone you meet is battling their own storm. You never know what simple word of encouragement or what random act of kindness might be just the spark they need to see their rainbow, to know their storm is ending and God is still in control.

So, I urge you: Go and live beneath that shimmering arch of color. Live with the hope, the trust, the strength, the joy that beautiful bow of promise brings. Go, and live the rainbow.

POINTS TO PONDER FOR
THE HUNCHED-OVER WOMAN

Read Luke 13: 10-17.

1. Even though much of the story is fictionalized, how does it compare to the story told in the scripture?

2. Does hearing the background of Lily help in understanding the scripture, knowing it was conjecture?

3. How did the support of her family help Lily deal with her disabilities?

4. What upsets you most about the way the people of her village treated Lily?

5. Why did the leader of the synagogue get so upset with Jesus' act of kindness?

6. What truly outraged Jesus about the leader's attitude?

7. In the story, what qualities of Lily do you most admire?

8. Are they consistent with what little scripture tells us about her?

9. Lily describes Jesus' feet as everyman's feet and His eyes as the eyes of her family. Do you think that reflects the universality of Jesus?

10. The story of the young girl is total fiction. Does it fit in with your image of Jesus?

11. Would you have ended it differently? How?

12. Do you agree with Lily's definition of the kingdom of heaven?

13. What gifts, talents, abilities or graces do you bring to the kingdom of heaven?

14. Think of time when you have received a kind word or a random act of kindness. How did it change your day?

15. How have you changed someone else's day by such a simple gift?

16. In what ways should we all "live the rainbow"?

MARY
THE MOTHER OF
CHRIST AT THE CROSS

John 19: 25-27

(Mary enters from off stage. She positions herself and looks up as if looking at a cross.)

This is the worst day of my life. In fact, it is the worst day in human history. You see, that is my Son dying on that cross up there. Oh, they tried to talk me out of coming. They told me no mother should ever witness the crucifixion of her son. Didn't they know? Couldn't they understand? I have to be here. For Him. I have to show Him that somebody still believes in Him, somebody still cares.

This must be the sword old Simeon warned me of all those years ago. With the first crack of the hammer on the nail I felt it enter my heart. Then, with each successive blow, it went deeper and deeper until with the last thud of the cross in the ground it had pierced my heart and soul through. Oh, my Son, my Son! How do you bear the pain?

So many memories come flooding back. I remember the day the angel came and told me I was to bear the Son of God. I was a mere child myself, so frightened, so overawed. What would the neighbors think? What would my parents say? And what of my beloved Joseph? How would he ever believe that which I could scarcely believe myself?

I became so frightened that I ran to my cousin Elizabeth, for it was rumored that she, too, was to bear a special child of God. I had half hoped she would tell me that I was wrong. That I had misunderstood the angel, or that I had imagined the whole thing. Instead, she confirmed what Gabriel had said: I was indeed to be the mother of the Messiah.

My soul soared and trembled. How would I, a poor peasant girl, ever accomplish such a magnificent feat? And why would Joseph, or any man, willingly choose to raise the Son of God?

But he did. He married me, and he stood by us all those years.

I remember the night He was born. We had had to travel from Nazareth to Bethlehem. Eighty miles on the back of that donkey, I thought my back would break. When we got there, poor Joseph could find no place for us to stay. I could have cried, but when I looked at his face, it looked as if he were about to burst into tears, as if he failed us or something, and I wouldn't hurt him for anything in this world. So, I smiled, and I told him that it would be all right, that God would provide, and on we went.

Finally, we found an innkeeper who allowed us to stay in his stables. They were warm and dry, and at least I could get off of that donkey. I looked forward to a quiet, peaceful night resting there in the sweet straw. Naturally, that was the night He chose to be born. It seemed so strange for the Son of God to be born there among all those animals.

Then, when I was so tired, tired to the very marrow of my bones, when all I wanted to do was to sleep with my newborn Babe in my arms, in come all these shepherds, sheep and all, to see the Baby. They told us some angels had appeared to them and told them to come and see the Son of God. Well, who was I to argue with angels?

I looked up at Joseph, and he was laughing. "Think of the stories we can tell our grandchildren," he said. He could always make me laugh. It was one of things I loved most about him. Oh, how I wish he were here with me now.

There were other visitors that first year also: Wealthy men traveling from far away bringing expensive gifts, long since spent on the necessities of life. However, they brought with them a warning also. They told us that Herod was going to try to kill the child; that we must get Him to safety. We left that very night for Egypt.

Later we learned that Herod did indeed try to kill our Son. He sent in his troops, and they murdered every child under the age of two. (*Cradling an imaginary baby*) Each time I held my own Babe, so soft, so sweet, so safe, my soul wept for the other mothers whose arms were empty and whose hearts were breaking because of Herod's hatred.

(*Slowly opening arms and holding them up*) And now, my own arms are empty, and my own heart is breaking because hatred is killing my Son, too! Oh, why does evil demand so much blood?! (*Covers her face in grief*)

I remember the years of His childhood. He seemed like such a normal child, so full of curiosity and mischief. Sometimes He would come running in, his eyes glowing, all excited over some creepy crawly thing He'd found under a rock. Sometimes He would come in with tears streaming down His cheeks because the other children had been teasing Him. Sometimes He would come in with His knees scraped and His tunic torn because He had been wrestling with the other little boys. Joseph and I would look at each other and wonder, " Can this truly be the Son of God?"

We were never really sure how much He understood about who He is and who is Father is. Not until that year He was twelve. We had gone to Jerusalem to celebrate the Passover. When we started back, I thought He was traveling with Joseph and the other men, and Joseph thought He was still with me and the women. It was three days before we realized He wasn't with either one of us. We went rushing back. Oh, I knew where we'd find Him, but I was so worried. You see, He had such radical ideas about God and the Law that I wasn't sure how the priests would react to Him.

When we got there, sure enough, there He was in the Temple, talking to the priests, asking questions, making comments. He looked up at us with those big wide innocent eyes of His and asked, "Why were you worried? Didn't you know that I would be here about My Father's business? "

It was the first time He'd given us any indication that He understood who He is and understood about His Father.

I remember the night Joseph died. (*Hugging herself*) Jesus took me in those strong, warm, comforting arms of His. He kept telling me, "It's all right, Mother, it's all right. He's finished his work here. He's gone home now. He's safe." Yet, even as He spoke those words of comfort to me, His tears mingled with mine because He loved His earthly father so. He kept saying, "I'll always be with you. You'll always have Me." And I always have, until now.

I remember the years of ministry: All the teaching, all the preaching, the parables, the miracles, the traveling, the crowds, the demands, the arguments, the challenges. Sometimes He would grow so weary of it we'd go apart, just the two of us, and we'd talk of lighter things. We'd talk about His childhood, of Joseph and His brothers and sisters. And we'd laugh. Oh, how we'd laugh. He had such a beautiful laugh, just like music.

But there is no music now, no laughter, only pain. (*Anger increases as she talks*) I look at my Son hanging there, His beautiful body beaten and bloody. A crown of thorns where there should be a crown of gold! I see Him dying there and my whole being fills with anger. I am angry at the disciples who have deserted Him. I am angry at the scribes and Pharisees whose hatred put Him there. And I am angry with God! Yes, with God!

I want to cry out to Him, "Where are You, God? How can You let this happen to Him? That is not just Your Son dying up there, that is my Son, too! I am the one who labored to bring Him into this world. I nursed Him. I bandaged His scraped knees and dried His tears. I let Him laugh and cry. I let Him be human and I am here for Him now, but where are You? I raised Him strong in the faith, and for what? For this? To die on a cross like a criminal for a world that doesn't even understand Him? Why? I would do anything in my power to stop this, but I can't. You could, but You won't. Is this the loving Father of whom He spoke so eloquently? Listen to Him, just listen. Do You hear Him? (*Pause as if hearing Jesus cry out*) He thinks You have forsaken Him and so do I. How else could You let this go on and on and on? Don't You care? Don't You feel anything? Where are You, God? Where are You?" (*Cries out and covers face*)

(*Take time to control emotion*) That is what I want to scream, but I can't. I can't. I know He does not need my anger or my doubts. He needs my faith and my love. And so, I stand here, watching this atrocity, and I say the only thing I can say. The same thing I have said all of my life. The same thing I have heard Him say all of His life, "Thy will be done, Lord. Thy will be done."

(*Hugging herself*) And suddenly, there is an arm around me. In that arm there is strength, and there is sorrow, and there is anguish. Somehow, I know that God is in that arm and that He, too, feels the agony. He, too, feels the grief.

I look at my Son there in the gathering darkness. With one last cry, it is finally over. My baby is dead. (*Again, sobbing and covering face.*)

(*Slowly look up*) And yet, on His face there is such a look of peace and (*pause as if looking for the word*) and victory, that I know this was indeed His destiny. He has finished what He was born to do. And I know, too, He is not my Baby; (*raising open arms*) He is truly the Son of God.

(*Slowly exit stage*)

POINTS TO PONDER FOR
MARY AT THE CROSS

John 19: 25-27

1. With which part of the story do you most identify?

2. Read Luke 2: 27-35. What did Simeon tell Mary which causes her to feel this was the "sword"?

3. Did Simeon's prophesies help prepare her for her role as mother of the Messiah?

4. How did Jesus fulfill all of what Simeon had said?

5. Read Luke 1: 39-56. Does Mary have any idea what the future holds for her Son?

6. During her stay, Elizabeth was a spiritual mother to Mary. Think of a time when a friend or relative have served as a spiritual parent to you. What did you learn from this person?

7. How have you been a spiritual parent to someone else?

8. How did that make you feel?

9. Mary feels the pain of the other mothers who lost children to Herod's hatred. How do you think she handled it?

10. How should you handle such feelings when faced with terrible tragedy?

11. Read Luke 2: 41-52. What did this incident teach Mary and Joseph about Jesus?

12. Why did they need this moment?

13. Mary's anger begins to build as Jesus continues to suffer on the cross. Why is she angry at the disciples? At the scribes and Pharisees? With God?

14. Mary shares Jesus' feelings of forsakenness. Did God truly forsake Jesus, or was He just being silent?

15. Have you ever been angry with God? How did you handle it?

16. Mary finally feels that God is sharing her grief which brings her comfort. How does it help knowing God shares your feelings, even if He doesn't act on it as you would wish?

17. Mary finally accepts that Jesus isn't just her son but is truly the Son of God. How does this realization change her relationship with Him?

18. How does recognizing Jesus as the Son of God change your life and your relationship with Him?

MARY
MAGDALENE

John 20: 1; 11-18

He is risen! Have you heard the news? He is risen indeed. Now, mind you, three days ago none of us believed we would ever be able to smile again, let alone be rejoicing like this. But maybe I should begin at the beginning.

My name is Mary. I am the one they call the Magdalene because of the little village from which I come, and I am one of Jesus' disciples. Yes, Jesus had female disciples. We traveled with Him, just like the men did. We learned from Him, just like the men did. And we served Him, like the men did. We, however, served in the, shall we say, more practical aspects of ministry. You know, things like food, clothing, places to camp. But Jesus always appreciated everything we did for Him, and He made sure we knew that we were just as important as any of the men.

Those were some of the reasons we loved Him so much.

As we started to make our way to Jerusalem, Jesus began to warn us about what would happen when we got there: How He would be betrayed, arrested, convicted on false charges, and then crucified. However, we mustn't despair because on the third day He would rise from the dead.

None of us really wanted to believe this. Oh, we like the part about Him rising on the third day, but as for rest of it? Who among us would ever betray Him, we all loved Him. And what had He ever said or done that could possibly warrant the death penalty?

But He was adamant about it. I remember Peter, one of His closest friends, took Him aside and started to chastise Him, "No, Lord, say it isn't so."

Jesus turned on him. He called him Satan. Told him to get behind Him. Then in a gentler voice He said, "Peter, Peter, you're thinking like a human being, you have to think like God." No one dared question Him after that.

When we got to Jerusalem, it was a day of celebration. Jesus rode in on the back of a donkey, the sign of a king coming in peace, and the people greeted Him as such. Oh my, they were waving palm branches, shouting, "Hosanna, God help us, Hosanna in the highest," and spreading their coats before Him as He came. We all thought, "Now surely, this is the way the Son of God should be treated."

But as the week went on, the whole atmosphere in Jerusalem began to change. Jesus began to openly attack the scribes and Pharisees, calling them hypocrites and condemning their kind of "religion." Then one day He did something that made us all wonder if the strain of ministry wasn't beginning to get to Him. He fashioned a whip out of three cords. He went into the Temple and started cracking the whip yelling, "My Father's house should be a place of prayer, but you have turned it into a den of thieves!" He overturned the money-changers table. People and animals scattered. Birds and coins were flying everywhere. Yet, under it all there was a calmness about Jesus. Somehow you knew this wasn't just a show of temper, He was preaching a sermon.

And the priests got the message, because that is when they truly started to plot against Him.

On Thursday, Jesus took His twelve closest disciples to room above where the rest of us were staying. The tension in our room was so thick you could have cut it with a knife. Mary, Jesus' mother seemed particularly agitated, as if she sensed something big was about to start. At one point we heard the door slam, and the sound of someone running down the stairs. I looked out, and there was Judas Iscariot, the treasurer of the group, scurrying off into the night. I couldn't imagine where he would be going at this hour.

Not long thereafter, Jesus and the rest of the men left. Mary came and asked me to follow them discreetly, so I could tell her what was happening. I was more than happy to do it, because I must admit my own curiosity was beginning to get the better of me.

I followed them to the Garden of Gethsemane where Jesus often went to pray. He left the eleven men in the outer garden, while He went to a more secluded place. I got as close as I could without infringing on

His privacy. I couldn't hear the words of His prayer, but the tone was unmistakable. It went from quiet conversation to pleading to an anguished cry, then silence. When He came out and saw that the men had fallen asleep, He looked so...so disappointed, and so terribly, terribly alone.

He tried to wake them, "Can't you even stay awake and pray with me this night?"

But the stress of the week, the heat of the night, and the power of the wine proved too much for them. They fell back to sleep. Jesus went back to the inner garden. There was more quiet conversation, more pleading, and a final cry of anguish. Then silence. Somehow, I knew that He had found the solace with His heavenly Father that He couldn't find with His earthly friends.

Jesus came back out and started to wake the men once more. That's when Judas arrived with guards from the Temple. He walked up to Jesus. Jesus looked at him with such pity on His face. "Judas," He said, " Must you betray me with a kiss?"

And he did. He kissed Him, and then all hell broke loose, and I do not use the term lightly. The men grabbed at Jesus. The disciples rose up in His defense. Peter grabbed a man's sword and sliced off his ear, his cry of pain rising above the mayhem.

Then above it all came Jesus' voice, " Peter, no! Stop it, all of you. He who lives by the sword shall die by the sword. "With that, He picked up the man's ear and put it back on. But even that act of kindness did Him no good. The guards grabbed Him and tied His hands behind His back. The disciples fled. One of the men shoved Jesus and He fell to the ground. He looked up, "Can't you even allow me the dignity of walking to my doom?" That just set them off. They started yelling at Him, kicking Him, spitting on Him. It was as if years of anger and frustration were being taken out on this one poor helpless innocent man. Finally, they pulled Him to his feet and started pushing Him out of the garden.

I waited until everything grew quiet, then I started to hurry back to the place we were staying. I had no idea how I was going to tell Mary.

When I walked in, there she sat, her hands busy with sewing, her lips busy in prayer. It was a scene we had all come to know and love. She looked up at me and her face blanched. "It's begun, hasn't it?"

I nodded. She pulled the cloth to her face and started to cry. I went and knelt next to her and started to cry with her. We held onto each other because there didn't seem to be anything else to hold on to. I don't know how long we sat there like that. Finally, Mary got control of herself. "Enough," she said, "No more tears, not until it's over. We must pray."

"Yes," I said, "We must pray for His safety and His release."

"No!" she said, "No, we must pray that He has the strength and commitment to finish what has begun, because if He fails, we are all lost!"

I had no idea what she meant, but I prayed just as she asked: not for His safety or release, but for His strength and commitment.

Finally, John came in. "They've taken Him to Caiaphas, but Caiaphas doesn't have the power to put a man to death, does he?"

Mary said, "Only God has the power of life and death over Jesus. Go back, both of you, find out what's happening and report back to *me*."

By the time we got to Caiaphas' house we learned that he had sent Jesus to Pilate. Now we were worried because Pilate did, indeed, have the authority to order a man crucified. When we got to Pilate's, we found he didn't want to have anything to do with this, so he sent Jesus to Herod. John went to Herod's palace, while I remained behind at Pilate's in case Herod sent Him back. I overheard a group of Pharisees talking. They were so proud of themselves. They had finally captured this radical Jesus. Finally captured Him? He had been preaching openly in the Temple every day that week. They could have arrested Him any time they wanted, but they were afraid; afraid of what the people would do. So, they waited until He was all alone in the middle of night. They were so sure they were going to get Him convicted of treason. Treason?!

What had Jesus ever said or done that could possibly be construed as treason? When asked about paying taxes He told us to render unto Caesar that which is Caesar's and unto God that which is God's. How can that possibly be treason? But they were so sure of themselves.

Finally, Jesus was brought back, because Herod didn't want to have anything to do with Him either, and he outranked Pilate. When they brought Him out, I couldn't believe my eyes. He had been badly beaten.

His face was swollen, His robe spotted with blood. The crowd's murmuring was growing louder, but Jesus just stood there silent as a lamb waiting for slaughter.

Pilate, to his credit, seemed to be hating this whole thing. He kept trying to give Jesus a way out, but He wouldn't take it. "They tell me you claim to be a king. Are you a king?"

Jesus answered, "My kingdom is not of this world."

"Now what is that supposed to mean? You do understand the seriousness of the situation, don't you? You know I have the power of life and death over you, don't you?"

"Any power you have comes from my Father."

"There you go again talking in riddles. Answer straight: Who are you, Jesus of Nazareth?"

Jesus looked at him with those steely eyes of His and asked him the question we must all answer some day, "Who do you say that I am?"

The crowd was clamoring for blood. In an effort to appease them, Pilate ordered Jesus to be flogged. Thirty-nine times the whipped cracked. Thirty-nine times the flesh tore and the blood flew. And thirty-nine times the crowd cheered. But still it wasn't enough for them. In a last-ditch effort Pilate brought out a convicted murderer by the name of Barabbas, because it was the tradition that that night one prisoner would be released as a show of good faith, and Pilate was certain the crowd would choose Jesus over a convicted killer. However, when he asked which one should be freed, the crowd chanted for Barabbas.

"What should I do with this man?" Pilate asked pointing to Jesus.

The cry came back, "Crucify Him!"

"No!!!" I screamed, but one small voice of sanity cannot be heard in a sea of madness.

"You would have me crucify your king?" Pilate asked.

Caiaphas, the chief priest, yelled back, "We have no king but Caesar." No king but Caesar? What of God? Is He not our Lord and King?

"But I find no fault in him," Pilate pleaded.

"Then let his blood be on our heads," Caiaphas said. As it truly is on all our heads.

Finally, Pilate realized he had lost, so he ordered Jesus to be taken away and crucified the next morning. Then, in a very public act of attrition, Pilate had a bowl of water brought out and literally washed his hands of the whole thing, as if that simple act could absolve him of all guilt.

I walked slowly back to the place we were staying. By the time I got there, John had returned and was seated next to Mary. She looked up at me and said one word, "When?"

"Tomorrow morning."

"Then we must go."

"No!" John and I both cried. "Ma'am," he said, "No mother should ever witness the crucifixion of her son."

She turned on him, "Don't you understand? I have to be there. For Him. He needs to know that He is not forsaken, that somebody still believes in Him. I must go, and go I shall, even if I go alone."

John and I looked at each other. We knew she was just stubborn enough to do it, but we also knew that we couldn't let her face this alone, so we agreed to go with her. Some of the other women came along. We went to the place where we knew He was being held and spent the night in prayer, again not praying for His safety or release, but praying for His strength and commitment.

When they brought Him out in the morning, I didn't think it would be possible, but He looked even worse than He had the night before. I don't know what kind of hell they put Him through in there. Someone had fashioned a crown out of thorns and had slammed it on His head so hard it had pierced His scalp. Blood had trickled down and dried leaving a horrendous pattern of lace. Jesus seemed blessedly unaware of what was going on around Him, until they threw that cross beam on His open bleeding back. He fell to His knees and cried out like an animal being sacrificed. Then began the long walk to Calvary.

The road was lined with people, taunting Him, mocking Him. The very same people who on Sunday had cheered Him as a conquering hero were now jeering Him to His death. Oh, how fickle we human beings are! John and I tried to block Mary's view, but she kept pushing us aside. She was going to witness this all.

At one-point Jesus fell. I pushed past the guards and ran to Him. I knelt down and wiped the blood from His face. He looked up at me and mouthed the words, "Thank you" before the guards pulled me away and forced Him to move on.

A little further up the road, He fell again. This time He simply couldn't get up. The guards pulled some poor man out of the crowd and forced him to carry the cross. As he walked up to Jesus, he looked at Him with such disgust. As he lifted the cross, Jesus looked at Him and said, "Bless you." The look on the man's face turned to one of awe and wonder. To be blessed for helping a man to his death seemed so wrong, but from Jesus it seemed so right.

When we got to Calvary, the sound of the hammer on the nails rang down through the valley as I knew it would ring down through all of history. At one point I felt my consciousness beginning to slip, but I looked at Mary and she was watching this all stoically. I thought, "If she can bear this, then so can I."

The thud of the cross going into the ground was like a death knell. Now, all we could do was watch and wait. Mary grabbed my hand. Every time Jesus cried out her grip would tighten. I thought my hand would break, but I felt no pain. All I could think about was the pain He was enduring.

Pilate had ordered a sign placed above His head. It read "King of the Jews " in three languages. Caiaphas was furious. "It should read He said He was king of the Jews!"

Pilate was adamant, " What is written stays." It is amazing how God can use even an unbeliever to proclaim the truth.

The crowd continued to mock Him. "Come on, Jesus, you've saved others, why don't you save yourself?

Why don't you call down that army of angels to help? I'd really like to see that. Or better yet, just step down off that cross. Come on, you can do it. Step down and we'll believe anything you say."

Jesus just looked up and said, " Father, forgive them. They don't know what they're doing."

Even one of the men dying with Him joined in the taunting. The other one quickly shut him up, "We deserve what we're getting, but not this man. Jesus, remember me when you come into your kingdom."

Jesus said, "Truly I tell you, today you will be with me in paradise." Even in death Jesus was bringing people to God.

Time seemed to lose all meaning as eternity hung there between heaven and earth. Finally, the sky began to darken, the wind began to blow, and the earth shook. Jesus looked up and said, "It is finished. Father, into your hands, I commend my spirit."

And He was gone.

Mary finally let go of my hand. I looked down. Her nails had dug so deeply into my flesh that I was bleeding, but I still felt no pain. I remember looking at her and thinking, "There are no tears. It must not be over."

Suddenly, she became all business. "Come, we must get His body. I have arranged for burial with Joseph of Arimathea."

John and I just looked at each other. "Ma'am," he said, "they are never going to give us His body."

"Yes, they will. Joseph has promised me he would arrange it."

What else could we do but to go with her? Sure enough, there were Joseph and Nicodemus, one of the Pharisees, talking with the guards. I don't know what was said, but they turned His body over to us. We took Him for burial in the tomb that Joseph was providing, but we didn't have time to properly prepare Him because Roman soldiers appeared and ordered us out. They had been given orders to seal the tomb and stand guard so quote, "You people don't try anything stupid."

You people. What did they expect us to do? We were a small band who had just lost our leader. Did they honestly think we would try to take on the whole Roman army?

I was about to tell them what I thought of their stupid order, when Mary shushed me. "It doesn't matter," she said, "Whatever God has planned will not be thwarted by these guards. Come. The Sabbath approaches. We will return when it has passed." With that, she kissed Him with the tenderness that only a mother can show. Then she covered His face with a cloth, and we left.

By the time we returned to the room in which we were staying, most of the other disciples had returned. The men told us what had happened in that upper room: how Jesus had taken the bread and after giving thanks, He broke it and shared it, telling them it was His body that was to be broken for us. After supper, He took the cup, and after blessing it, He shared it telling them it was His blood that was to be shed for us. He said that we should always remember that in the breaking of His body and the shedding of His blood a new covenant was being formed, a covenant that would last forever. But what did it all mean? What did any of it mean while Jesus lay in that dark, sealed tomb?

That room was filled with fear and trembling. Every time we heard a noise we jumped. Every time we heard footsteps in the street, we were afraid the soldiers were coming to take us away. We really didn't know what to do. Should we stay together, or would it be safer if we were to split up? And the question above all questions hung there in the air, almost visible, but unspoken for fear of the answer: will He rise on the third day, or have we truly followed a fool?

Late that night, Peter returned. He looked like a man haunted. He didn't say a word to anyone, not even his wife. He simply went and sat in a corner his back to the room. Peter being silent was something none of us was used to and it simply added to the eeriness of the room.

The next day was spent much the same way. We were afraid to stay and afraid to go. We were truly like sheep without our shepherd.

By the evening of the second day an eerie silence fell over the room as we each became lost in our own memories of Jesus.

I remember when I first met Him. I had been possessed by seven demons. They made me do terrible things. I had heard that Jesus was driving out demons and I wondered if He were powerful enough to handle seven at once. I went to hear Him preach. I was very impressed. I was just beginning to work up the nerve to ask Him if He could help me when I felt the demons beginning to stir out of the dark pit in my soul in which they dwelt. I tried to fight them down, but they were too powerful. They took control and started yelling at Him, horrible obscene things.

He turned and looked at me. Oh, it was my voice, but it was their words. He started walking towards me. The demons got angrier and angrier. When He got close, they began to kick dirt at Him. When He came even closer, they spit on Him. He raised His hands. I thought He was going to hit me, but instead He grabbed my shoulders and looked into my eyes.

"Mary!" He said. (*Each Mary should be said quieter and with more compassion.*)

The demons paused, startled by this turn of events. I tried to cry out, "I'm here. Please help!" but by then the demons were back in control.

"Mary!" He said a second time, and the smallest weakest demon fled. It gave me hope and I started to fight.

"Mary," He said a third time, and another demon was gone.

"Mary," He said a fourth and fifth time, and more demons were gone.

"Mary," He said a sixth time, until finally only the biggest, strongest and most hate-filled demon of all remained.

"Mary," He said a seventh time, and this demon that could stand up to all the hate and abuse aimed at it fled in the face of compassion and grace.

"It wasn't me! It wasn't me," I cried.

"I know. It was the demons, but they're gone now."
I searched through that dark pit in my soul, but it was
empty. "Yes," He said, "they're gone, but if you don't
find something with which to fill that void, they will
return, and they will be even more powerful than
ever."

Well, I knew exactly what I was going to fill that
void with: I was going to fill it with Him. So, I became
one of His disciples. At first, I really didn't feel like
I belonged there. Oh, it's not that anyone was ever
unkind to me, they weren't. It's just that my past
was so different from theirs. How could any of them
understand from where I had come?

Then one night I was sitting on the fringe of the
camp, as I always did, when Jesus came and sat down
next to me. I don't know how He managed, but He
always seemed to find time to spend one-on-one with
us just when we needed Him most. That was really the
biggest reason we loved Him.

He sat down and started talking to me about
His childhood and His relationship with His father
Joseph. He told me about all the things He used to
do to test His father's resolve. Nothing really bad,
just the things all children do to test their parents'
limits. He chuckled, "I knew I could do it because I
trusted his love for me. And he never let me down. He
never lowered the bar, nor changed the rules. After
an incident was over, the punishment accepted and
the lesson learned, he never brought up to me again. I
often wondered about that, so one day I asked him.

"'What is the point?' he said, 'the past is the past. It
cannot be changed or altered in any way. And I loved

you in the past, for the past is what made you who you are today. And I love who you are today. But what is more important is who you be tomorrow. I will love you tomorrow no matter what, but I want you to be the very best person you can be. That is why I will never lower the bar nor change the rules. Rather, I will do everything in my power to help you reach the bar and to understand the rules.'"

"That's the way it is with God. Your past is your past. It cannot be changed or altered in any way. God loved you in the past because the past made you who you are today. And God loves who you are today. But what is more important is who you will be tomorrow. God will love you tomorrow no matter what, but He wants you to be the very best person you can be. That is why He will never lower the bar nor change the rules. Rather He will do everything in His power to help you reach the bar and understand the rules."

Suddenly, I knew I was right where I was supposed to be in the middle of the Kingdom with all the other forgiven sinners.

Sometime during the night, I fell into a fitful sleep. The sound of the hammer on the nails echoed in my dreams and the thud of the cross going into the ground jarred me awake. In the first few moments when dreams still held sway and reality fought for its proper place, I thought, "This is the third day. This is the day that will prove if He is Messiah or if we have indeed followed a fool."

As reality won the battle, I realized that what I thought had been the cross going into the ground was actually the sound of the door closing. Someone had left. I looked around and saw that Mary was gone. I knew exactly where she was going. I knew, also, that I couldn't let her face this alone. Not only because I was afraid of what the soldiers might do to her, but because of what might happen if He hadn't risen from the grave.

I left the room and quietly closed the door behind me. As I made my way to the garden the sunrise was more glorious than ever. I remember thinking, "How can the sun be rising so beautifully when the light of the world is gone?"

When I got to the garden everything was very quiet. There was no sign of Mary anywhere. As I approached the tomb, I didn't see the soldiers there, either. I was afraid they had arrested Mary and taken her away. However, as I got closer, I saw one of the men had dropped his sword and shield. Now, no Roman soldier would ever leave his sword and shield behind when arresting a prisoner.

As I approached the tomb, I realized that the stone had been rolled away. Surely, the soldiers wouldn't have done that for Mary. I went and looked in. As my eyes adjusted to the darkness, I saw that His body was gone. The cloth that had covered His face was rolled up neatly and placed at the head and I thought, "Yes, Mary's been here, but where has she gone? And what has she done with His body?"

As I stood there puzzling about it, I heard a voice outside the tomb, "Um, excuse me, but for whom are you looking?"

Between the darkness of the tomb, the brightness of the dawn and the tears that filled my eyes, I didn't recognize Him. I thought he was a gardener. "Please, sir," I said, "They have taken the body of my Lord and I don't where they put it. If you show me where it is, I will go and care for it."

Then He said one word. He said, "Mary." (*With the same tenderness used with the seventh demon.*)

I turned and I saw Him. His handsome face had been totally healed. His whole body had been made whole. There was nothing left of the ordeal He had been through except the scars in His hands, His feet and His side; eternal reminders of the depth of God's love and the length to which He is willing to go to save us.

"Rabbi," I cried, and I ran to Him.

"Mary," He said, "Mary, you mustn't cling to me like this. There is so much to do, and I have such little time left on earth. Go back. Tell the others what you have seen. Tell them to wait for me and I will join them when I am able."

I didn't want to leave either Him or the garden, so I tried to argue with Him. "But they'll never believe me."

He just smiled, "Peter will."

I knew then that whatever had happened, Jesus had forgiven Peter and He would find a way to make Peter forgive himself.

So, I ran. I ran all the way back to where we were staying. I burst into the room with the glorious news. "He is risen," I cried, "for I have seen Him!"

For the first time in two days, Peter came out of that corner. He came up to me and said, "Woman, are you sure?"

"Yes, Peter, I'm sure. I saw Him. I spoke to Him. He told me we should wait here and that He will join us when He is able."

Then Peter looked at me with such pleading in his eyes, "Did He say anything else?"

"Yes, Peter, He told me that you would believe me."

"He's done it!" Peter cried and picked me up and twirled me around. Then he and John went running out to check the tomb, because I'm not sure they actually did believe me.

Soon they were back. "Mary's right, the tomb is empty. There's nothing there but His grave clothes."

Now the room was filled with joy and wonder. What did it all mean? When will we see Him again? What's going to happen next?

Suddenly, despite the locked and barred door, Jesus was standing in middle of us, smiling and greeting us with the same greeting He always used, "Peace. Peace be with you."

Then the party really began in earnest. Oh, we still had many questions, but now we had the answers. Sometime during the celebration, I looked at Mary and there were tears streaming down her cheeks, but these were tears of joy. I thought, "There are the tears. It must be over."

And, oh, my dear brothers and sisters in Christ, it is over. The long dark night of doubt and despair has ended for the Son has risen gloriously and eternally.

The war with evil is over. Oh, the battles will continue for Satan is not easily discouraged, but it doesn't matter. The victory has been won. Satan did the worst he could: He killed God Himself, but he couldn't keep Him in the grave. Jesus has broken the gates of hell. Never again will death have the final say.

Because He lives, we too shall have eternal life if we only accept the gift He so graciously offers.

So, I urge you, go and meet the living Lord. Walk with Him. Learn from Him. Accept the gift He so graciously offers so that you can join me in assuring a weary world, "He is risen, for I have seen Him."

Amen.

POINTS TO PONDER FOR
MARY MAGDALENA

John 20: 1, 11-18

1. Nowhere in scripture are we told anything about Mary's past, simply that Jesus drove out seven demons. What type of person do you think Mary was before her encounter with Christ? How was her life changed?

2. We don't necessarily believe in demon possession today. What type of behavior might have been attributed to demons for which we have other explanations? (i.e. Drug addiction, alcoholism, depression)

3. Can Jesus help with these?

4. Think of something in your life which may separate you from God. How can faith help in this struggle?

5. Mary didn't feel she belonged with the other disciples at first. Have you ever felt that way?

6. How did you handle it?

7. What are some things you could do to make someone else feel comfortable in a strange situation?

8. Mary comes to terms with her past when she realizes the truth of God's forgiveness and her chance for a new and better life. Is there something in your past you need to let go of, knowing God has forgiven you?

9. How will that help you move ahead?

10. In the scene describing the crucifixion, which part touched you most? Why?

11. When they leave Jesus' body in the tomb Mary says, "It doesn't matter. Whatever God has planned will not be thwarted by these soldiers." Is this a statement of hopeless resignation or undeterred faith?

12. What do you think went through the minds of the disciples between Jesus' arrest and His resurrection?

13. Has there ever been a time in your life when you have had doubts about your faith? How did you handle it?

14. We are never told where Jesus' mother was the morning of the resurrection. Where do you think she might have been? Why?

15. Mary admits to not wanting to leave Jesus in the garden, but she goes to tell the others even though she fears they won't believe her. Have you ever been in a situation where you did something you didn't want to do simply because you felt God was calling you to do it? What were the results?

16. How are you joining Mary in telling the world, "He is risen"?

PETER'S MOTHER-IN-LAW

Mark 1: 29-31

Good afternoon. My name is Ruth. Now I know what you're probably thinking. You're probably thinking I'm that other Ruth; the one that has that whole section named after her in your collection of scriptures. What do you call that collection again? The Bible. That's right, the Bible. I should be able to remember that: Basic instructions before leaving earth. Well, I am not that Ruth. That Ruth was generations and generations before me. I am, however, mentioned in your scriptures. I get about that much mention. *(Holding thumb and index finger about an inch apart.)* I'm not even mentioned by name. That use to depress me, but then I thought about all the hundreds of people with whom Jesus interacted, all the lives He changed that aren't even mentioned at all, so I suppose getting even that much mention *(holding them again)* is saying something.

Now the reason I get even that much mention *(again holding the finger and thumb apart)* is because of my son-in-law Simon. You probably know him better as Peter. As a matter of fact, Simon was not even supposed to be my son-in-law. You see, when my daughter Abigail reached the age to be married, my husband David decided the perfect man for her would be Joshua, the local rabbi. Needless to say, Abigail was less than enthusiastic about this choice, and she began to pout in the way only a teenage girl can pout. She moped around the house. She whined while she did her chores. Her feet dragged everywhere she went, and surliness just radiated from her.

Now David, to his credit, did not want to force her into a marriage she truly didn't want, so he went on an all-out campaign to prove to her what wonderful man Joshua is and what a truly great husband he would be. The main thrust of this campaign was for me to prepare and serve dinner while they sat around and talked all night.

Poor Abigail was bored out of her mind. The evening would begin with the sighs. (*give a bored sigh to the left and right.*) Every time Joshua said something, he thought was humorous, her eyes would roll. (*Roll eyes and grunt*) Next the yawning would begin; stifled at first. (*give a stifled yawn.*) Then not so stifled. (*give a full yawn.*) Finally, she would plead a headache and go to bed.

This went on for some time until finally I began to notice a change in my daughter's attitude. There was a sparkle in her eyes. She was singing while she did her chores. There was a little dance in her step, and she was volunteering to run errands for me.

Now David, bless his loving little masculine heart, was sure his plan had worked, and she had finally come to realize what a wonderful man Joshua is and what a truly great husband he would be. But as her mother I had the sneaking suspicion there was another explanation behind this sudden change in my daughter's attitude. So, one night as we were doing the dishes, I very subtly broached the subject.

"All right, dear, who is he?"

(*Looking innocent*) "Who is who, Mother?"

"Who is the man who put the sparkle in your eyes, the song on your lips, and the dance in your step?"

"I don't know what you're talking about, Mother."

"Come on, Abby, I have had that same sparkle, that same song, and that same dance. Now who is he? It's not Joshua is it?"

"Oh, Mother, really!"

"Well, what's the matter with Joshua?"

"Well, nothing I guess, but he's so boring. I mean, all he ever talks about is the Law."

"Of course, he talks about the Law. He's the rabbi, what do expect him to talk about?"

"Well, I don't think Joshua even truly understands the Law. I mean, I don't think God gave us the Law as a strict set of rules of dos and don'ts, but rather as guidelines to help us in our relationship with Him and our relationships with each other."

Now, those were some pretty deep thoughts coming out of my daughter's head, and I wondered who had put them in there, so I went on. "You know, Abby, your father has his heart set on you marrying Joshua."

"Oh, but I don't love him!"

"Love? What's love got to do with it? We're talking marriage here, girl. If you're lucky, love comes later."

"Oh, you just don't understand!"

(*As an aside*) Right. I've never been a teenage girl. "Well, if it's not Joshua, then who is he?"

She hemmed and she hawed, and she blushed a little bit until she finally came out with, "Simon, bar John."

"Simon! The fisherman?!"

"Now, Mother, don't be snobbish. Fishing is a perfectly honorable profession."

"Well, I know that, dear, but a fisherman?! Abigail, how do you ever expect to get your father to agree Simon would make a better husband for you than Joshua?"

"You could help."

"Yeah, well I don't know if I think Simon would make a better husband for you than Joshua."

"That's because you don't know him. The least you could do is to meet him."

Well, she had me there. So, I agreed that I would go with her and at least meet this Simon bar John with whom she was so infatuated.

Early the next morning found us on the shores of the Sea of Galilee. There was such pride on Abigail's face as she pointed out Simon's boat, but she didn't have to point out which of those men was Simon. I knew who had captured my daughter's heart. He stood head and shoulders above the other men. He had stripped down to his waist, his muscles were large and firm and brown from hours of hard work in the hot sun. He had an air of authority about him. When he barked out on order the men jumped to obey, but he wasn't above getting down and dirty right alongside rest of them. At one point the nets began to slip, and he let out such a string of obscenities. I just stared at Abigail.

"Oh, he never talks that way around me."

"Well, I would hope not! Abigail, how do expect to get your father to agree to have Simon to dinner, let alone marry him?"

"Oh, you can do it, Mom. You can talk Daddy into anything!"

Now where does the child get these ideas? I mean, in our house the man is lord. What he says goes. If David says Simon is not coming to dinner, then Simon is not coming to dinner. End of discussion.

So, the next week when Simon was coming to dinner, I was a bit nervous. I had the sneaking suspicion the only reason David had eventually agreed to this was so he could show Simon up and prove to Abigail that Joshua was indeed the better man.

Right at the appointed time there was a knock at the door. I opened it, and there stood Simon looking very, very nervous. You could tell he had gone to a great deal of trouble to make himself look good, and he cleaned up quite nicely. In his hands he held a bouquet of wildflowers. Something about the idea of this big burly fisherman taking the time to pick wildflowers for my daughter touched my heart.

Then he held them out and said, (*In a deeper voice*) "Here, Ma'am, these are for you." And my heart melted.

The evening went far better than I ever imagined it would. David did use every opportunity to bring up Joshua's name, but Simon handled it quite well.

"Yes," he said, "good man, the rabbi, good man. I'm not really sure he truly understands the Law, however. You see, I don't think God gave us the Law as a strict set of rules of dos and don'ts, but rather as guidelines to help us in our relationship with Him and our relationships with each other."

Hmmm. Now where have heard that before? I looked over at Abigail, and she was absolutely enthralled by every word coming out of Simon's mouth. There was no sighing that night, no eye rolling, and no yawning stifled or otherwise.

By the end of the evening, we had become quite impressed with this Simon, bar John. Here was a man who obviously thought about a lot more than just fishing. He became a frequent visitor after that. He led us on some lively discussions. We became quite fond of him, so when he asked for Abigail's hand in marriage, we willingly turned her over to his keeping.

It was a decision we never regretted. Simon was a good husband, and when the children started coming along, he was a good father. Oh, you knew fishing was important to him, but you also knew it was only the means by which he supported his family. They always came first. You see, those whom Simon loved, he loved passionately, and that which he believed, he lived fervently. Theirs was a home that was filled with love and laughter and faith.

Life was good.

Then tragedy struck. My beloved David died. Now in my day, widows didn't have very many options. We couldn't own property. We couldn't get a job. We were pretty much dependent on the men folk in our lives, so I reluctantly moved in with my son and his family. It was awful. They treated me like an unpaid servant. I was expected to work, and I worked very hard, but I was never invited to join in any of the family discussions or decisions. I was expected to care for the children, but I was never allowed to discipline them, and those children needed disciplining, believe you me. I was miserable.

Then one day while I was visiting Abigail, all of my loneliness and frustrations came out in a torrent of tears. That night, as I sat alone in my corner, I began to feel guilty. What did I really have to complain about? I have a roof over my head and food to eat. Many widows lack even these simple necessities. I was trying to figure out what to say to Abigail by way of an explanation and apology when all of a sudden, the door flew open and there stood Simon, filling the door frame.

(*In a deeper voice*) "Get your things, Mother, you're coming to live with us."

My son started to stand up in protest, but Simon yelled, "Sit down, you. Mother is absolutely miserable living here, and I don't blame her. You treat her like some kind of a slave, and I won't have her living like that."

We all knew that when Simon was in that kind of mood, you did not argue with him. He helped me gather my few belongings, threw my bed over his back, grabbed me by the hand and off we went. It was wonderful. Oh, I still worked very hard, but now I was one of the family, welcomed to join in the discussions and the decisions. I was given free hand to both love and spoil my grandchildren. Life was good once more.

Then He entered our lives. He was a traveling rabbi from Nazareth by the name of Jesus.

Simon's brother Andrew first took Simon to hear Jesus preach. Andrew had been a follower of John, the one that had been baptizing, but he said this Jesus was the one John had been prophesizing about.

That first day Simon came home all excited.

(*In a deeper voice*)"This is a man who talks about God in a way I can relate to. He talks about a God of love, not of law; a God of grace, not of judgment; a God of mercy, not of vengeance."

Everyday Simon would go and hear Jesus preach, and every day he would come home more excited. Abigail and I began to worry. Oh, the fishing business never suffered, and he did come home to his family every night, but we had never seen Simon react this way to any of these traveling rabbis before. He usually just dismissed them out of hand, but he was becoming absolutely obsessed with this Jesus.

Then one day he came home more excited than ever. "You'll never believe what happened," he said. "We'd been out fishing all night; hadn't caught a single thing. So, I decided we might as well bring the boat in and get some rest. As we approached the shore, Jesus was standing there. He hollered out, 'Any luck?' 'Yeah,' I yelled, all bad. 'Well, why don't you cast the nets on the other side of the boat? 'Huh, I thought. What can this carpenter from Nazareth teach me about fishing? But we hadn't had any luck any other way, so I figured we might as well try, and maybe I could teach him a thing or two about humility. So, I ordered the nets cast on the other side of the boat. They no more than hit the water than I began to feel a tug. It got heavier and heavier. The nets began to tear. I had to call James and John over to help get the catch on shore. When we did, there were hundreds and hundreds of fish there; all different kinds, sizes, shapes and colors flopping around in the hot sun. And there in the middle of it stood Jesus, laughing right along with the rest of us.

"Then he looked at us and got serious. He said, 'Follow me, and I will make you fishers of souls. Our catch will make this one look miniscule.'"

Abigail and I held our breaths. Simon continued, "You know, I would love to follow him. I would love to see what kind of a difference this man is going to make in this world, but I can't leave my family."

Abigail and I both sighed a sigh of relief, yet we knew Simon was being torn apart by his desire to follow Jesus and his love for his family. No man should have to live divided like that.

That's when I became very, very ill. I was running a high fever. The world was becoming very dark and blurry. People were nothing more than blobs walking around, voices muffled and unintelligible. I knew I was being pulled towards that dark abyss of death. I didn't really mind. I'd had a good life. My parents had wanted me. My husband had loved me. I had seen my children grown and watch them be established in homes of their own. I had held my grandchildren and watched them as they grew. The only thing I truly regretted was that I never got to meet this Jesus who's coming had so excited Simon. My last thought as I went over the precipice was, "I wonder if He really will make as big of a difference in this world as Simon seems to think He will." With that I fell into the dark void.

I don't know how long I was there. The first thing I remember was someone calling my name. I didn't recognize the voice. It was tender, yet insistent. As I came up out of the darkness into the gray light of dawn, I felt hands on my cheeks and forehead. They were cool and gentle yet calloused from hard work. I opened my eyes, and I saw Him. Somehow, I knew this must be Jesus.

He smiled at me. "Welcome back, Ruth, "He said and helped me sit up. He sat down next to me and gave me some wine. "How are you feeling?"

I thought about it. "I feel fine."

"Good," He said, "Because I need your help."

He needs my help? This man who just brought me up out of the dark abyss of death needs my help? What could I possibly do for Him?

He explained, "Simon wants to follow me, and I want him as one of my disciples. He already has a better understanding of God and the Law than most men, but he needs training. Training he can only get with me. But Simon will not leave his family. Now what I need is for you and Abigail to convince him that you are perfectly capable of handling the fishing business, so he is free to follow me."

I just stared at Him, "But we don't know anything about the fishing business!"

"Oh, you'll learn. Zebedee will help. His sons James and John are coming with me, also. He'll teach you everything you need to know. If I didn't think you could do it, I wouldn't even ask. My Father would never want a family left destitute just so someone could follow me. Think about it. Discuss it and give me your answer in the morning."

Well, I promised Him that we would indeed discuss it, and we did. Abigail and I talked about it all that evening as we prepared and served dinner. While we were serving, a sudden thought hit me. "Abigail," I said, "What day is this?"

She thought about it a minute and said, "Why, it's the Sabbath." Then she started to giggle, "Can you imagine what Joshua would say if he knew we were cooking and serving on the Sabbath?"

"Why, he'd be furious!" And I started to giggle.

Out of the corner of my eye I caught Jesus watching us. When I looked at Him, He gave me a little wink, and He started to chuckle. I thought, now here truly is a man who is more concerned with the spirit of the Law than He is with the letter of the Law.

After they left, the three of us, Simon, Abigail, and I sat down and we talked about what Jesus had asked. We listed all the pros and cons, but sometime in the wee small hours of the morning, Abigail and I realized we had lost Simon to a better man. Then, just after dawn, amid tears of sorrow and excitement, Simon left to follow his destiny.

Well, Abigail and I did learn all there is known about the fishing business. Zebedee was a great help. I now know more about fish and fishing then I ever wanted to know in my whole entire life! But we made a success of it. We made enough to not only support the family in the style to which we had become accustomed, we made enough to help support Jesus in His ministry. Every time they were in the area Simon would come home filled with stories about all the things he'd seen, and learned, and done. And Jesus would always come with him. He'd make sure to take Abigail and me aside and tell us how very proud He was of us, and how much He appreciated our sacrifices for His ministry. It meant a lot.

Every year we would go to Jerusalem to celebrate Passover with them. I will never forget that final year.

We had gone up early to spend more time with them, so we were there when Jesus entered the city. Oh, what a day of celebration that was. Jesus rode in on the back of a donkey, the sign of a king coming in peace, and the people greeted Him as such. They were waving palm branches, shouting, "Hosanna, God save us, hosanna in the highest" and throwing their cloaks on the ground before Him.

But as the week went on, the entire atmosphere of Jerusalem began to change. Jesus began to openly attack the scribes and Pharisees, calling them hypocrites and condemning their brand of "religion" Then one day He did something that made us all wonder if the strain of ministry wasn't beginning to get to Him. He fashioned a whip out of three cords. He went into the Temple and began cracking the whip yelling, "My Father's house should be a place of prayer, but you have turned it into a den of thieves!" He overturned the money changers table.

People and animals scattered. Birds and coins were flying everywhere. Yet, under it all there was a calmness about Jesus. Somehow, you knew this wasn't just a show of temper, He was preaching a sermon. And the priests got the message, for that is when they truly started to plot His demise.

On Thursday, Jesus took His twelve closest disciples, Simon among them, to the room above where the rest of us we are staying. Later they told us what had happened up there. Jesus had taken the bread, and after giving thanks and blessing it, He broke it and gave it to them telling them it was His body that was to be broken for us.

Likewise, after supper, He took the wine. After giving thanks and blessing it, He shared it telling them it was His blood that was to be shed for us. But in the breaking of His body and the shedding of His blood a new covenant was being formed: a covenant that would last forever.

Late that night Jesus and the disciples left. The tension in the room where we were staying was so thick you could have cut it with a knife. Mary, Jesus' mother, seemed particularly agitated, as if she sensed something big was about to start.

Then very late that night the disciples began trickling in, and with them, a horrible story began to unfold.

Jesus had taken the men to the Garden of Gethsemane where He often went to pray. While there, Judas Iscariot came in with guards from the Temple. They arrested Jesus and took Him to Caiaphas. With as bad as that news was, we knew Caiaphas did not have the authority to put a man to death.

But then more disciples returned, and the story got worse. Caiaphas had sent Jesus to Pilate. Now we were worried because Pilate could indeed order a man crucified.

Then came the worst news of all. Pilate had given into the pressure from the priests and populace and had ordered Jesus to be crucified the next morning. Mary, John, and some of the other women decided to go and show their support for Him. Abigail and I remained behind.

You see, I had witnessed other crucifixions, and I simply couldn't bear to watch someone I love die, like that. And besides, Simon had not yet returned. We knew how impetuous he could be, and we were afraid he would try to mount a one-man rescue operation.

The hours seemed to crawl by. Sometime during the next day, the sky began to darken, the wind began to blow, and the ground shook. It is said that that was the exact moment in which Jesus died. It is also said that at that exact moment the cloth in the Temple which separated the Holy of Holies was ripped from top to bottom as if God Himself was rending His cloak in grief.

Towards sundown, Mary and the others returned. Somehow they had gotten possession of Jesus' body and had taken it to a tomb provided by Joseph of

Arimathea for burial, but they hadn't had time to properly prepare Him because Roman soldiers had arrived and ordered them out. They had been given orders to seal the tomb and stand guard so, quote, "you people don't try anything stupid." What did they expect us to do? We were a small band who had just lost our leader. Did they honestly think we would try to take on the entire Roman army? Yet, Abigail and I both knew it was something Simon just might try.

That room was filled with fear and trembling. Every time we heard a noise we jumped. Every time we heard footsteps in the street we wondered if the soldiers were coming to take us away. Should we stay together, or would it be safer if we split up? And the question above all questions hung there in the middle of the room, almost visible, but unspoken for fear of the answer: Will He rise on the third day, or have we truly followed a fool?

Finally, late that night, Simon returned. He didn't a say a word to anyone, not even to Abigail. He just went over and sat in a corner, his back to the room. He pulled his cloak up over his head as if he wished he could disappear. Never in all my born days have I seen so large a man look so small.

Abigail went over and knelt down next to him. "Simon," she said, "Simon, what's wrong? What's happened?"

"It's over," he sighed, "It's all over."

"No," she said, "No. Don't you remember what He said? He told us this would happen. He told us He would be betrayed, arrested, and crucified, but He also said that on the third day He would rise from the dead. Don't you believe Him, Simon? Don't you think He can do it?"

"Oh yes," Simon said, "I believe Him. I believe everything He ever said. I believe He will rise on the third day and He will go on and establish His church. But it doesn't matter, because it's all over for me."

"But why, Simon? Why?"

"Because," he sobbed, " because I betrayed Him."

"No," she cried, " No. It was Judas Iscariot who betrayed Him, not you."

"No, I betrayed Him, too. I swore that I would go to my death with Him. And I tried, Abigail, I truly tried. I followed Him to Caiaphas, but there in courtyard, three different times three different people asked me if I knew Him, and every single time I denied even knowing Him. It was exactly what He said I would do."

"Oh, but you were frightened. He'll understand. He'll forgive you."

"Oh, I know He'll forgive me, but it doesn't matter. It's still all over for me."

"But why, Simon, why?"

"Don't you understand?" he cried. "I was Peter. I was the rock on which He was going to build His church and I broke. How can He build His church on a broken rock?" And he started to weep.

Abigail looked to me for some words of comfort, but I had none to give. This was something God was going to have to work out with Simon on His own.

The next day was spent much the same. We were afraid to stay and afraid to go. We were truly like sheep without our shepherd. Towards the evening of the second day an eerie silence fell over the room as exhaustion began to take its toll.

Then, just after dawn on the third day, Mary, the one they call the Magdalene burst into the room with the glorious news. "He is risen," she cried, "for I have seen Him."

For the first time in two days, Simon came out of that corner. He went up to her and said, "Woman, are you sure?"

"Yes, Peter," she said, "I'm sure. I saw Him. I spoke with Him. He told me we should stay here, and He will join us when He is able."

"Did He say anything else, "Simon asked with such pleading in his eyes.

"Yes, Peter," she said, "He told me you would believe me."

"He's done it!" Simon cried and picked her up and swung her around. Then he and John went rushing out to check the tomb, because I'm not sure they really did believe Mary. Soon they were back. "Mary's right. The tomb is empty. There's nothing there but His grave clothes."

Now the room was filled with joy and wonder. What did it all mean? When we see Him again? What's going to happen next?

Then suddenly, despite the locked and barred door, there in the middle of us stood Jesus, smiling and greeting us with the same greeting He always used, "Peace. Peace be with you."

Now the celebration started in earnest. Sometime in the middle of it, Simon and some of the other disciples left. We didn't know where they had gone, but Jesus knew. Later Simon told us what had happened.

Simon did what he always did when he was upset and needed to think; he went fishing.

"Yeah," he said, "We'd been out all night. Hadn't caught a single thing, so I figured we might as well bring the boat in and get some rest. As we approached the shore, there was a fire going and man standing next to it. He hollered out, 'Any luck?' Yeah, I yelled, all bad. 'Well, why don't you cast the nets on the other side of the boat?' That's when I knew it was Jesus.

"I dove out of the boat and swam to shore. I stood before my Lord naked, physically and emotionally. He took off his cloak and wrapped it around me. When the others got there, He prepared fish for us. When we had finished eating, He took me aside. 'Simon,' He said, 'do you love me?'

'Yes, Lord, I love you.'

'Then feed my sheep. Simon,' he said a second time, 'do you love me?'

'Yes Lord, I love you.'

'Then feed my lambs. Simon,' He said a third time, 'do you love me?'

'Oh, Lord, You know my heart better than I do. You know how much I love you.'

'Then feed my sheep.'"

Three times Simon had denied knowing Him and three times Jesus allowed Simon to declare his love for

Him. In that remarkable moment of emotional healing Jesus took that failed fisherman and turned him to a successful shepherd. For the rest is, as they say, history.

Simon was a cornerstone of the early church. Jesus took that broken rock and put him together again with mortar made of His own body and blood; a mortar nothing can ever shake apart. I have often thought that his own failure made him a much better leader because, indeed, he knew firsthand how easy it is to fall. But he also knew firsthand the forgiving grace of the living Lord. Abigail joined him in his ministry. And me? I stayed home and took care of the fishing business, still making enough to not only support the family, but to also to support the early church.

I wept when I learned both Abigail and Simon had been martyred for their faith. It is said that Simon insisted on being crucified upside down because he felt unworthy to die in the same way as his Lord. I believe it. It is something Simon would do. For as I said, those whom Simon loved he loved passionately, and that which he believed he lived fervently.

Simon's name and deeds are known down through the annals of history. Mine are known only to God. But that is all that really matters. You see, a church is not built with cornerstones alone. Rather, lesser stones are needed to build the walls, and the Master Builder will reject no stone which is offered to Him. It doesn't matter how big you are, or how small you feel, Jesus has a use for you. It doesn't matter if you are smoothly polished, or a little rough around the edges, Jesus knows just where you belong. It doesn't matter if you conform nicely to the stones around you, or you are rather oddly eccentric, Jesus knows just where you'll fit. He will place you there with that same precious mortar of body and blood to build His church eternal; a church that not even the powers of hell will be able to bring down.

So, I urge you, give yourself to the Master Building. Let Him place you where He sees fit. Serve Him to the best of your ability, so that someday you, like Simon, and like me, will hear those wonderful words, "Well done, oh good and faithful servant. Come and share in my glory."

Amen.

POINTS TO PONDER FOR
PETER'S MOTHER-IN-LAW

Read Mark 1: 29-31

1. Although scripture tells us nothing about Peter's relationship with his mother-in-law, how do these verses show his affection for her?

2. Because it was the Sabbath, Jesus had been teaching in the local synagogue. Yet, when Peter's mother-in-law was healed, she got up and served them. Why was this so shocking? Why didn't Jesus object?

3. Peter is called to leave his family and business behind to follow Jesus. What factors lead him to make this difficult decision? What factors have influenced you when faced with life changing decisions?

4. Although scripture tells us nothing about what happened to Peter's family, in this story his wife and her mother keep the family together and help support the ministry of Jesus. How important is family support in ministry?

5. Jesus appreciates all their sacrifices for His ministry. Do you feel your efforts and sacrifices are appreciated?

6. How do you show your appreciation for those who aid you in your service?

7. In this story, Ruth and Abigail don't attend the crucifixion. Does this show a lack of faith or commitment to Jesus?

8. After his denial of Jesus, Peter cries that it is all over him. What does he mean? Have you ever felt some failure has ruined your relationship with Jesus? How can you regain the previous relationship?

9. When Mary brings the good news that the tomb is empty, Peter and John rush to check. Did the empty tomb dispel all their doubts? Why or why not? Do you ever doubt the empty tomb? How do handle that doubt?

10. Read John 20: 19-22. Jesus appears to the disciples in a locked room. He greets them with the word peace. After all that had happened, why was this an appropriate greeting? How did it allay their fears?

11. Read John 21: 1-8. Why didn't Peter and the others recognize Jesus at first? Has there ever been a time in your life when Jesus was with you and you didn't recognize Him? How did He make Himself known to you?

12. Peter was the first one out of the boat and swam to Jesus. Do you think it took courage to approach Jesus alone after denying Him three times? Do you have such courage to approach Jesus when you have failed Him?

13. Read 1 Peter 2: 4-7. Where do you see Jesus placing you in His church of living stones?

PHOEBE

Romans 8: 28-38; 16: 1-2

Good morning. My name is Phoebe. I must confess
that I always get a little nervous when I am invited
to tell my story because I really don't think I have
ever done anything very remarkable. You see, I have
never had to overcome any great obstacles in my life. I
have always been blessed with good health. I've never
needed a miracle. Oh, I believe in miracles. I've seen
them happened, but I, thank God, have never needed
to be on the receiving end of one. I didn't have to pull
myself out of crushing poverty. As a matter of fact,
my father was a very successful businessman. He had
money, position, influence and sons. The only minor
obstacle I ever faced was being a woman in a society
which looked at us as second class citizens. Even that
wasn't a big problem because my father never looked
at me that way. After five sons he was delighted to
have a little girl.

"Phoebe," he used to tell me, "God created humans
male and female; each with their own intelligence,
their own abilities, their own desire to seek Him, their
own curiosity and their own wisdom." Then he would
chuckle, "Perhaps a little too much curiosity for Eve

and not enough wisdom for Adam. But remember, Phoebe, God has a plan for you just as surely as He has for any of your brothers; a plan to give you a future with hope. He has your name inscribed in the palm of His hand just as deeply as any man."

Because of my father's radical ideas I was tutored right alongside my brothers. I learned history and literature, mathematics and science. I was taught not only how to run a household, but also how to run a business. I blossomed in my education. My business sense was even better than most of my brothers. Father used to say, "Phoebe, it is a shame society insists upon looking at the clay pot instead of the heart and soul which resides within. In so doing, they miss the remarkable person you truly are."

When I began to reach adulthood, my thoughts turned to marriage. I had my heart set on my childhood friend Chuza. He was the very epitome of everything I thought a man should be, a veritable reincarnation of our great King David. He was tall and handsome, educated and ambitious. Chuza wanted to be a steward in King Herod's palace, to dwell in the halls of power. I wanted to be right there by him, a helpmate and confidant. I thought that dwelling in the palace would make me feel like a princess.

However, Chuza had eyes only for my friend Joanna. My heart broke when my dreams became her reality.

Father tried to comfort me. "Phoebe," he said, "I would never have given my permission for you to marry Chuza anyway. His heart is so set on gold and position that he has no room left to love a woman. I am sure God has a much better man in mind. Always remember, Phoebe, even when God does not act as we wish He would, He always acts in our best interest. Believe that and it will carry you through good times and bad."

So, hope began to flicker in my broken heart thinking that if God had a better man than Chuza in mind for me, he must be someone truly extraordinary. But my heart broke again when my father announced whom he had chosen for my husband: Ezra.

Now don't misunderstand, there was nothing wrong with Ezra. He was a highly respected business associate of my father's, but he was almost twice my age! Much more a contemporary of my father than of me. He was a widower whose wife had been unable to give him children. I was afraid he was looking at me as a housekeeper, a bed warmer, or a breed mare, or worse as a delicate little porcelain doll to be brought out and admired but never actually touched. However, I had always been taught to honor my father and part of honoring is to trust and obey, so I buried my dreams in the rubble of my broken heart and married Ezra without complaint.

(*Slowly begin to smile*) It was the first time I truly understood the truth of my father's adage that even when God does not act as we want Him to, He always acts in our best interest. Ezra was a wonderful husband. He never thought of me as housekeeper or bed warmer or breed mare, and certainly not as a delicate little porcelain doll only to be admired. Because he respected my intelligence and my business sense, he thought of me as a partner bringing me into all aspects of his business. As a matter of fact, Ezra was far more interested in matters of theology than of economics, so he joyfully turned over the running of the business to me and Eleazar, our chief steward. We did him up proud. The business flourished under our leadership. We had holdings all over the Roman Empire.

Everywhere we went Ezra would tell me, " Phoebe, my jewel, we will be meeting people who do not believe the way we do. You see, they worship a god of gold instead of the God who created gold. That does not mean, however, that they are evil or ignorant. They simply don't know about our God. Often, we will see shrines to an unknown God. That God, Phoebe my jewel, that God, is our God. It is up to us to teach them about Him. However, that doesn't mean looking down on them, or arguing with them, or treating them as unworthy and certainly not by violence, but rather by our actions we show them what a good and gracious God He is, and what a joy it is to serve Him. Remember, Phoebe my jewel, God is the God of all people, even if they don't recognize Him as such."

Ezra truly lived what he believed. He treated everyone the same. It didn't matter how rich or poor, how powerful or humble, what nationality or what beliefs they held, Ezra treated them with respect and grace. For the most part, people returned that respect, and because of our relationships to him, Eleazar and I also received that same response. Business was booming.

Ezra looked at all our blessings in a different light than most people. "Phoebe, my jewel," he would tell me, "God has truly blessed us, but He did not give us all this for our own benefit. No, He blesses us so we can pass on those blessings to others."

That was the way he lived his life and did business. Often, he would say to me, "Phoebe, my jewel, that man we hired today seems so gaunt and underfed. Phoebe, my jewel, our table is always so weighted down; surely we could spare some food for him and perhaps send some home for his family."

I would smile, "Yes, of course we can, Ezra." At lunch time all our workers received some extra rations, and a special "wage package" was sent to the man's home. That night as I lay safe in my husband's arms, my heart was warmed by the thought of children sleeping soundly because they did not have to listen to the growling of empty tummies.

Ezra was especially aware of the plight of the least, the last and the lost. "Phoebe, my jewel," he would say, "Look at that woman over there. She just lost her husband. Look at her cloak. It is so threadbare. It will not keep her warm this winter. Phoebe, my jewel, your closet is overflowing; surely you have a cloak you could give to her."

I would smile, "Yes, Ezra, of course I have. You know, I have a friend who is expecting yet another babe. She is already so overwhelmed with those she has, let me make a few inquiries and see what I can do."

After a few well place conversations I knew that the woman was not only wrapped in the warmth of a new cloak, she was wrapped in the warmth of a new family.

Like my predecessor, I also was unable to give Ezra children. That did not mean, however, that our house was devoid of their laughter and life. Many times, while we were out Ezra would say to me, "Phoebe, my jewel, look at that little urchin over there. Her rags barely cover her body. She is digging through the garbage for something to eat. Phoebe, my jewel, surely, we can find room for her in our household. We must protect that little lamb from the wolves."

"Of course, we have room for her. We can always use more help in the kitchen." (*as an aside*) or the garden or the stables, according to the gender of the urchin. So, another child would join our household. However, there were certainly responsibilities which came with living under our roof. The most important of which was getting an education.

"Education, Phoebe, my jewel," Ezra would say, "Education is what will bring a brighter future, a future with hope to these children."

So, every morning the children would be required to take lessons from Ezra. But it was hardly a chore. Ezra was a wonderful teacher, because he taught from the heart. When a child left our home, he did indeed leave for a better life.

Although we owned houses all over the Roman Empire, home was truly Jerusalem. Not only because that was where the Temple was, but because Ezra loved the multiculturalism that was found there. He loved inviting the most diverse of people to gather around our dinner table.

Sometimes, the discussions would begin to get a bit heated, and when they did, Ezra would call to me, "Phoebe, my jewel, come here and pour your sweet oil on these troubled waters. Gentlemen, listen to the wisdom of my wife and learn the truth."

Many of the men would secretly scoff at the thought of a woman having any opinion worth listening to, but out of respect for Ezra they would welcome me into the conversation. As I talked you could almost feel the animosity in the room begin to dissipate.

One of the men we enjoyed entertaining most was a zealous young Pharisee from Tarsus by the name of Saul. Oh my, Saul was a Pharisee among Pharisees. He knew every Law and prophesy word by word and letter by letter. He could find the exact statement he needed to support any theory or belief he had. The problem was that although he knew exactly what the Law and prophets said, he didn't seem to understand the love which God expressed through them.

"Saul," Ezra would tell him, " You are so on fire for the Lord, but you burn with a fire which destroys everything it touches. Phoebe, my jewel, come here and teach our young friend about the fire which warms and purifies."

The first time he called me in I was scared. I knew what I believed the Law and prophets said, but unlike Saul, I couldn't just quote an exact passage to support my opinion. However, after our first encounter I realized I could match Saul point by point, argument by argument and I began to enjoy our debates.

Saul, on the other hand, never believed a woman was capable of understanding the deep meaning of scriptures and was upset by my insights. The angrier he got, the more amused Ezra was. "Saul, my young friend, someday God is going to pick you up, turn you upside-down and shake out all those false ideas you have. Then, He will fill you with His true fire, that fire of grace and glory, and you will be an unstoppable force for Him. I only hope I am there to see it when it happens."

Saul would get in snit and leave in a huff, slamming the door as he went but a week later, he would be back for more discussions. However, in all our discussions, I could never change Saul's opinions, and he could never change mine. Still, we came to respect each other in spite of our differences, and we truly enjoyed our debates.

It was while we were living in Jerusalem that I learned even more emphatically the truth of my father's adage that even when God doesn't act as we wish, He always acts in our best interest. You see, as happy as I was with Ezra, that was how miserable Joanna was with Chuza. Living in the palace wasn't like being a princess at all. The palace was a place of intrigue and immorality, backstabbing and deceit. Joanna had always been prone to fits of extreme moods, going from ecstasy to deep depression in an instant. Living in a place where you couldn't trust anyone frequently sent her into times of madness.

Chuza would bring her to our door, "Phoebe, please, Joanna is acting up again. Please get her calmed down. People are beginning to talk. She is endangering my position."

I wanted to scream at him, "Are you more worried about Joanna or your precious position?"

But Ezra sensing my fury would step in, "Phoebe, my jewel, go and prepare a cup of your special tea. Chuza, you return to the palace. We'll send for you when Joanna has recovered."

Yet, even after we got her calmed down, the spark of madness would remain in her eyes. As we returned her to Chuza and the palace I knew it wouldn't be long until she was back in that pit of despair.

One night Ezra and I were awakened to the sound of someone kicking our door. It was Chuza. He could barely contain Joanna as she struggled in his arms. Her eyes were wilder than I had ever seen.

"Phoebe," Chuza said, "This is worse she's ever been. Please, do something with her!"

I looked at her, "Joanna, Joanna, what's wrong? What's happened?"

"His eyes," she cried, "They're still staring, still judging! But the blood! It's everywhere! They think he's dead, but those eyes still see! Soon he will open his mouth, and he'll condemn us all to hell!"

I looked at Chuza, "What is she talking about?"

"You know that prophet John? The one who has been baptizing out by the Jordan and talking about the kingdom of God being near? Well, he openly condemned Herod for murdering his brother because he lusted after his brother's wife. Herod had him arrested, but even he didn't have the courage to execute an acknowledged prophet of God.

"Then tonight the power of the wine and the sensuousness of Salome's dance sent Herod over the edge. He foolishly promised her up to half his kingdom. Under the orders of Herodias, she requested the head of John the Baptist on a silver platter. In order to save face, Herod had to order his execution. Joanna was there when his head was brought in, and this is the result.

"Phoebe, if you can't get her calmed down, I'll have to have her chained in the dungeon. She will cost me my job if she continues to act like this."

I wanted to scream, "You would chain her in the dungeon? Why don't just take her out of the prison you already keep her in?"

Ezra spoke, but there was an edge in his voice I rarely heard, "Phoebe, my jewel, go make an extra strong cup of your special tea. Chuza, leave her here and go back to your precious position. We'll take care of your wife." With that, he practically pushed Chuza out the door slamming it behind him.

When we finally got Joanna calmed down and asleep, Ezra said, "I cannot understand any man loving his position and his wealth more than his wife."

I looked at him and I realize that Ezra would sacrifice everything he had for me. I began to cry, "Oh Ezra, my love, forgive me. Please forgive me."

He took me in his arms. "Of course, I forgive you, Phoebe, my jewel. With my whole heart I forgive you. Just tell me one thing: for what am I forgiving you?"

I looked at him. There was such honest confusion and concern on his face that I began to laugh and cry at the same time, "Oh, Ezra, forgive me for ever having reservations about marrying you. You have been the best husband any woman could ever have. I am truly blessed."

He smiled, "If I am to forgive you, then you must also forgive me, for I had my own reservations about marrying you. I didn't think I would ever be the husband you deserved. Isn't it wonderful how God worked to bring us together in spite of our foolishness?"

At that moment, I knew I would never love another man the way I loved Ezra.

Sometime later, Joanna came to our door alone. I noticed right away there was something different about her. The madness was gone from her eyes. There was a peace and joy about her I had never seen before.

"Oh, Phoebe," she cried, "I've met Him!"

"Whom have you met?" I asked.

"I've met the Messiah!"

"Oh really? The Messiah? Who is He?"

"He's a carpenter from Nazareth named Jesus, and He is wonderful!"

"A carpenter from Nazareth? How do you know He's the Messiah?" I asked as I tried to keep from laughing in her face.

She said, "I was in one of my periods of madness. I was wandering around Jerusalem with some other women when we came upon Jesus. He took one look at me and knew just what to do.

He drove the demons out of me. Oh, Phoebe, for the first time in my life I feel whole. I'm finally free!"

I misunderstood, "You've left Chuza?"

"No. I wanted to. I wanted nothing more than to follow Jesus and help to support Him, but He told me I could serve Him much better staying where I am and witnessing to those in the palace who truly wish to seek God. However, Chuza hasn't even noticed a difference in me. He still thinks I get periods of madness. He just lets me come and go as I please. Whenever Jesus is in Jerusalem, I can go to Him and learn and help. Phoebe, for the first time in my life I have the freedom you have always enjoyed with Ezra!" She was practically giddy with joy.

I said, "I'm really happy for you, Joanna. I would love to meet this Jesus. Next time He is in Jerusalem we must have Him to dinner."

"Oh yes," she said, "You and Ezra would love Him. He explains things so well. I'll make sure you know when He is back."

When she left, I looked at Ezra and started to laugh, "A carpenter from Nazareth is the Messiah?"

But Ezra wasn't laughing, "Phoebe, my jewel, we must pray that we are not among the fools who expect God to act in ways we anticipate. We both know that His plans are high above ours, His ways different than ours. My biggest fear is that when the Messiah comes, He will not come as the mighty warrior we all expect, but rather as the suffering servant or the good shepherd. Phoebe, my jewel, we must pray that when the Messiah comes we recognize Him whether He is the great warrior king, the strong gentle shepherd, or a carpenter from Nazareth."

I knew that my husband was right.

As Passover approached, Ezra's health was beginning to decline. I was especially worried when the day came we usually went to the Temple to give our tithes and offerings. It was always a joy for him because he loved to watch the people as they gave, but this day Ezra decided to remain in bed. "Phoebe, my jewel, you must go and present our offerings for us both."

"Oh no, Ezra," I protested, "I want to stay with you. I'll send Eleazar. He can do it for us this once."

"Phoebe, my jewel, you have been everything Lemuel says a wife should be. Please this one time do as I ask: take our offerings and be my eyes and ears at the Temple. Come home and tell me all the things you see. "

When he put it like that, what else could I do?

The Court of the Gentiles was filled that day. People had come from all over to celebrate Passover in Jerusalem. The sound of coins being thrown in the golden trumpets was at times deafening as people tried to outdo one another to show how much they had given. I saw Joanna with a group of people, and I figured one of them had to be Jesus, but they all seemed to be just so common. However, there was one ordinary looking man, who had the most extraordinary eyes. He was watching everything that was going on and seemed to see things no one else could see. I followed the direction He was looking and saw a poor old woman going up to give her offering. Her widow's weeds were thin and worn. She must have been wearing them for years. She looked as if she hadn't eaten in sometime, as if a strong breeze would blow her away. However, there was such a look of joy on her face as she went forward. She dropped two small coins into the trumpet. They were so small they didn't make any noise at all. Suddenly, her face became radiant. It was almost as if she were in the very presence of God, but that in His presence there was no fear or trembling, only contentment and peace.

At that point that ordinary man with the extraordinary eyes said, " Fellows, did you see that? That woman over there just gave the most wonderful gift."

The men looked at Him like He was crazy, "What do you mean? She only gave a couple of small coins."

"Is that all you saw? Don't you understand? God doesn't care about money. She gave much more than anyone else here. She gave her heart. She gave her love. She gave her very soul. She gave because she wanted to be part of the kingdom of heaven. That is a gift truly pleasing to God."

Suddenly, Joanna and the other women swooped down on the poor widow and began to lead her out. I chuckled thinking that she may have come into the Temple alone, but she would never be alone again.

At that moment I caught another transaction out of the corner of my eye. A young couple was trying to offer two pigeons as a sacrifice to redeem their infant son. The priest was telling them, "Oh no. These pigeons aren't good enough."

The young man said, "But we raised them ourselves. They're the best we have."

The priest said, "Then your best isn't good enough for God." At that point I saw a flash as the priest slyly pulled a small knife from his sleeve and pricked one of the pigeon's breasts. "You see," he smirked, "this bird is not perfect. Now, you would not have the audacity to offer an imperfect sacrifice to a perfect God, would you? You will simply have to buy two of the birds we've raised here in the Temple."

The young mother looked like she was about to burst into tears. "But we have no money. We've spent everything just to get here."

At that point I knew something had to be done. I rushed over, "Oh, what beautiful pigeons. Look how big and plump their breasts are. Oh please, I know it is asking a lot, but would you sell them to me? My husband is not feeling well and I'm sure a broth made from these birds would do him a world of good."

Before they could answer I dropped enough coins into the young man's hand to cover the cost the Temple birds plus some extra to help them get home. However, the priest grabbed every coin. "This will be sufficient. Now we can redeem your son."

The anger burned even hotter in my heart. I looked at the mother, "What a beautiful baby. May I hold him?" She handed him to me and I said, "May God bless you, little one, and may you always seek the future He has planned for you; a future with hope." When no one was looking I slipped some more coins into the boy's swaddling clothes so I knew the family could get home safely.

As they left and I began to gather my pigeons I heard a voice behind me, "What a kind and gracious thing you did. "

I didn't look around but said, "Oh, those priests just make me so mad! It is bad enough how Rome exploits us, but that is understandable because they serve a god of gold. These priests, however, are supposed to serve the God who created gold. Instead, they keep putting up stumbling blocks for those who wish to come to Him. Can't they understand that God is not so much concerned with the sacrifice, but rather with the heart that is offering it?"

Suddenly I was afraid I had spoken out of line, but I heard the man chuckle, "I couldn't have said it better myself."

I turned and there was that ordinary man with the extraordinary eyes looking at me. "I'm Jesus and you must be Phoebe."

I was surprised He knew who I was, but then it clicked, "Oh, yes, Joanna must have told you about me."

With a mischievous glint in His eyes He said, "Yes, that's it. Joanna told me about you."

I said, "She's been telling my husband Ezra and me about your preaching. We would love to have you come to dinner some night. My husband just loves discussing theology."

He said, "I would like that very much, but with this being Passover week, I'm afraid I'm a little busy. Could we make it next week?"

I said, "Yes, next week would probably be better."

He smiled, "Then next week it will be. I'll see you then." As He began to leave, He suddenly stopped and looked at me, "Phoebe, do you truly believe that even when God does not act as we want Him to, He always acts in our best interest?"

I said, "Yes, yes I do."

"Good. Hold on to that faith, for it will serve you well in good times and in bad."

I thought: What an odd thing to say.

When I got home, the meaning of that last statement became the most important lifeline I've ever had. You see, sometime while I was at the Temple, my beloved Ezra passed from this world. Grief came crashing over me like a tidal wave. I struggled just to take one breath after another. What was I to do? How would I manage without his guidance? How would my heart ever keep beating without his love? The world had suddenly become dark and fearsome. I knew big things were happening in Jerusalem, but I didn't know what and I really didn't care. Nothing mattered except my emptiness.

Joanna came to visit, but she was crying out her own pain. It seemed that Jesus had been crucified and they had buried Him. She kept asking me what it meant, what she should do. I couldn't answer her because all I could think was: another false messiah. What did it matter anyhow?

When she finally left, I looked at Eleazar, " I can't deal with any more visitors. I need to grieve alone. Please, Eleazar, just send everyone away until I'm ready to face the world again." I retreated to my darkened room and wondered if the light would ever shine again.

I don't know how many days had passed. People came and went, but Eleazar honored my request and let no one bother me. One day, however, he came in, "Mistress, you have a visitor."

"Eleazar, I told you I don't want to be disturbed."

"Yes, Mistress, but I really think you need to see this man."

"Eleazar... "

"Mistress, haven't I always been a good and faithful servant? Have I ever disobeyed your orders? This once, could you trust that I have your best interest in mind and honor my request?"

I looked at him and knew he was right. "All right, Eleazar, I'll come, but not because you have always been a good and faithful servant, but because you have always been a good and faithful friend."

When I went out, the visitor was looking out a window. The light of the late afternoon sun surrounded Him with a warm glow. "Welcome to my home."

He turned and there were those extraordinary eyes looking at me, but He didn't look very ordinary anymore. "I believe we had a dinner engagement planned for after Passover," He said with that mischievous look in His eyes.

My mouth must have dropped open, "But Joanna said You had been crucified!"

"Oh, a minor inconvenience for a major accomplishment."

"But she said they had buried You!"

"They did, but I found I didn't like being in the tomb. It was too dark and cold, and that stone slab was very uncomfortable, so I left." When He saw how confused I was He became serious, "I am alive, Phoebe, and because I live, Ezra lives also."

"Ezra's alive? Where is he? I must go to him at once!"

"Phoebe, Phoebe, you don't understand. Ezra is alive, but not in this world. He is with my Father. He is patiently awaiting his radiant jewel."

"I don't understand." I started to cry.

"I know it is difficult. Why don't we have dinner and I'll try to explain it all to you."

That's just what we did. My whole household ate with us and Jesus answered all our questions, and even some we didn't think to ask! When Jesus was about to leave, He did the most unusual thing: He breathed on us all. As I inhaled His sweet breath I felt my despair turn to hope, my fear turn to faith and my emptiness turn to purpose. As He lifted His hands in blessing I saw my name and the name of every member of my household inscribed in the palm of His hands right next to the scars from the nails.

He said, "Peace. My peace I leave with you, and remember, I will be with you always." With that He left.

It wasn't long before the persecution of the church began in earnest. One of the most zealous of the persecutors was Saul. He came to visit one day, breathing fire, "I can't believe it, Phoebe. They actually think this carpenter from Nazareth is still alive. "

"He is."

"No He isn't. I saw Him die on that cross. I saw Him buried in that tomb. I don't how they did it, but they got His body out and I know it is somewhere just rotting away.»

"No it's not. I've seen Him."

"No, you saw someone who looked like Him."

"No, Saul, it was He. He was here. I saw the scars in His hands. We ate together. Believe it, Saul. Jesus is the Messiah."

"I didn't hear that! For the sake of my old friend Ezra I didn't hear that. But I warn you, Phoebe, if you ever utter that nonsense outside this house, I'll come back and arrest you and your entire household!" With that he left and slammed the door.

I looked at Eleazar, "He will, too. We must leave at once."

We went to my favorite villa in Cenchrea, a seaport near Corinth. I was amazed at how much the people had heard about what was happening in Jerusalem. Because they knew I was from there, they kept asking me all about Jesus and the new church. I answered as best as I could, but I felt I needed help. I wrote to some of my friends and asked for someone to come and help.

One day I opened the door and there stood Saul. I said, "I can't believe you have come all the way from Jerusalem just to arrest me and my household, Saul."

He looked down at his feet, "I'm not Saul, I'm Paul."

"A subtle difference," I huffed.

He looked up into my eyes, " No, a major transformation. Do you remember how Ezra used to tell me that one day God was going to pick me up, turn me upside-down and shake all my wrong ideas out of me? Well, it happened, Phoebe, on the road to Damascus. I was struck down by a blinding light. A voice came out of it, 'Saul, Saul, why are you persecuting me?' Well, I had no answer. For three days I was blind, but in my blindness, I finally saw the light. I know that Jesus is Messiah, and I have dedicated my life to serving Him. But I need your help, Phoebe."

I couldn't help but needle him a little, "The great Sau... I mean Paul needs the help of a mere woman?"

"I deserved that," he said, "But yes I do. You are already a leader in the church of Corinth. In Jerusalem you would be known as a deaconess. I need you to help me get a foot in the door; to help them to accept me and my authority."

What could I do but help him? We became great partners working together. We resumed our old debates over dinner, but now he could change my mind and I could even occasionally change his!

One day he came to me, "Phoebe, the church in Rome is beginning to grow, however they need guidance. I am unable to go at this time, but I have written a letter. I need someone to deliver it; someone who knows my mind and my beliefs. Someone who can answer any question just as I would answer them. That someone is you. Will you take this letter to Rome for me?"

I was astonished, "Me? Oh, Paul, they would never accept me."

"I have already written an introduction for you. They will accept you as my emissary."

"But I don't want to go to Rome. I don't like Rome!"

"Aren't you the one who always says that even when God doesn't act as we want Him to, He always acts in our best interest? Is your dislike a good enough excuse to let souls hungry for the bread of life starve?"

(*As an aside*) Don't you hate it when your own words come back to haunt you?

Well, I couldn't argue with him, so off I went. I guess that is the one remarkable thing I ever did in my life: I was Paul's emissary to the church in Rome.

That's my story. I hope somewhere in it you heard something that touched your soul. If nothing else, I hope you leave believing that even when God doesn't act as we want Him to, He always acts in our best interest. Or as Paul more eloquently put it: all things work for good for those who love the Lord and are called according to His purpose. May you truly believe that He has your name inscribed in the palm of His hand and seek the future He has for you, a future with hope. If you never have an encounter with Christ as dramatic as Paul did, may you at least feel His breath. As you inhale His sweetness, may your despair turn to hope, your fears turn to faith, and your emptiness turn to purpose. God give you peace, and remember, He is with you always.

Amen.

POINTS TO PONDER FOR
PHOEBE

Read Romans 8: 28-39; 16: 1-2

1. In this story, Phoebe is treated equally with her brothers. How important is it to remember that God sees value in all people?

2. How do you reflect that belief in your dealings with others?

3. Phoebe says she never had to overcome any great obstacles. What obstacles do you see her overcoming in this story?

4. Are there things in your life you have overcome that seemed small to you but may have seemed great to others?

5. What role did your faith have in the situation?

6. For Phoebe, not winning Chuza was a great disappointment. What has happened in your life that has been a major disappointment?

7. How did you handle it?

8. Marrying Ezra turned out to be a great blessing for Phoebe. When in your life has a situation seemed to be bad, but turned out good?

9. What are some qualities of a Christian life do you see exemplified in the lives of Phoebe and Ezra?

10. Ezra sees more in Saul then his narrow understanding of the Law. Has anyone ever seen more in you than you see in yourself?

11. How has that helped encourage you?

12. The scene in the Temple tells the story of the widow giving her last two coins. Why was this gift so noteworthy in Jesus' eyes?

13. Why did the priest's actions infuriate Phoebe?

14. Was her intervention a good way to handle her anger?

15. Read Proverbs 32: 10-21. How does Phoebe, as described in this story, reflect what this passage says about a good wife?

16. How can these qualities be applied to church leadership?

17. Why did Paul need Phoebe's help both in Corinth and Rome?

18. What does it tell us about women's role in the church?

19. Has your encounter with Christ been a dramatic one like Paul or a quiet inhaling of His breath like Phoebe?

20. How has your life changed because of it?

CPSIA information can be obtained
at www.ICGtesting.com
Printed in the USA
BVHW030300170120
569258BV00001B/1